Richard Randolph Michaux

Sketches of Life in North Carolina

Embracing Incidents and Narratives, and personal Adventures of the Author during

forty Years of Travel

Richard Randolph Michaux

Sketches of Life in North Carolina
Embracing Incidents and Narratives, and personal Adventures of the Author during forty Years of Travel

ISBN/EAN: 9783337209698

Printed in Europe, USA, Canada, Australia, Japan

Cover: Foto ©Andreas Hilbeck / pixelio.de

More available books at **www.hansebooks.com**

PREFACE.

It is known by many that the writer has had it in mind for several years to write a book of sketches and incidents of his travels in North Carolina, having seen both sides of life from the Blue Ridge to the Atlantic coast, and of late a number of friends have asked, "where is the book you were going to write." Well, here it is. It is not claimed to be a literary work, but the thoughts of the writer given in the best English he can command; and his aim is not to give a complete account of events, but to present subjects and incidents as memory may bring them up for illustration; and they are not fictions of the imagination, but facts drawn from real life. So these sketches will embrace a little of history, geography, autobiography, &c. Humorous readers will find amusement in a number of incidents related. Dr. Talmage says all healthy people laugh, but if any are too pious to laugh, or whose liver is out of order, they need not read the book. But it will contain many wholesome and instructive truths, which will bear criticism in the light of the Scriptures. But yet it may not escape criticism, for the purest Being who ever walked this earth was hated, and finally put to death, for speaking the truth; and all those who follow his example will offend those who do not love the truth

I cannot promise, as did a N. Carolina author, who some years ago wrote a poem abounding in strong satire. In his introduction he said:

"Fair ladies, never, never fear:
God bless your souls, I love you dear:
Therefore I'll spare you all I can,
And mostly try my luck with man."

But in the course of the poem he made some reflections on the fair sex, and, recollecting himself, immediately apologized, saying;

> "Then be at ease, take no affright,
> For fear you'll burst, you're laced so tight."

But my motto is, to "shoot folly as it flies," whether it flies high or low, "sparing neither age, sex or color." "What I have written I have written," and so submit it to one and all, hoping that the Author of all truth will make it useful to some.

THE AUTHOR.

Contents.

PAGE.

CHAPTER I..................................... 9
    Introductory.

CHAPTER II.................................... 13
    Retrospection—Emigration to North Carolina—Early Experiences—Schools and School Masters, &c.

CHAPTER III................................... 21
    The Darkey as I have seen him in North Carolina—His ruling traits and his religious character—Some noted ones.

CHAPTER IV................................... 32
    Preachers and preaching—Some preachers of a generation ago—Funeral preaching—Anecdotes of preachers—Self conceit.

CHAPTER V.................................... 43
    Illiteracy—The Bible, and mistakes about what is in it—A remarkable Bible reader—Homemade Scripture—Misquotations and perversions of the word.

CHAPTER VI................................... 54
    Superstition—Belief in Witches—Conjuration—Spells, &c.—Other humbugs.

CHAPTER VII.................................. 65
    Religious denominations in N. C.—Camp Meetings—Some differences between Eastern and Western N. Carolina—Anecdotes of preachers.

CHAPTER VIII........ 78
    Hospitality—Incidents illustrating character—Some contrasts—Dogs in N. Carolina—The dog at church.

CHAPTER IX........................... 86
    Romance in real life illustrated—Some Temperance stories which illustrate the cause of Strong Drink—Some cases beyond the reach of Keeley.

CHAPTER X................................... 92
    Marriages in North Carolina—Laws and customs concerning it defective—Primitive marriages more rational—The clergy officiating on such occasions a relic of Romanism.

CHAPTER XI 97
    Marriage itself—Some comments and suggestions—Some illustrations.

CHAPTER XII............................... 107
    The public roads in North Carolina—How some people give directions to travelers—Quaint names of some localities—Some personal adventures, and curious characters met with.

CHAPTER XIII............................. 118
    Some other curious characters and things noted—Life, and how they live, in the two extreme sections of North Carolina, contrasted.

CHAPTER XIV............................. 131
    Lost in a mountain gorge, in a pitch dark rainy night—A preacher in an awkward predicament—More personal experience—An extraordinary "Fish Story," &c.

CHAPTER XV.............................. 143
    Some experiences in the mountains about the

close of the war—Evading a controversy—Incidents of the Prohibition campaign of 1881.

CHAPTER XVI........................... 150
The status of Christianity in N. C.—How far, as a people, are we Christianized?—The optimistic and the pessimistic of things.

CHAPTER XVII........................... 161
Hindrances to the advancement of Christianity in our own country—The follies and vices of society at the present day.

APPENDIX.

CHAPTER I............................... 184
The Romish hierarchy identified as the great Anti Christ of Revelation—The whole system shown from the Scriptures to be false—Its intolerance and persecutions.

CHAPTER II.............................. 213
Romanism in our own country—More light turned on the subject—The pope in our politics—No real Catholic can be a true citizen of our Republic—Some historical facts showing the influence of Romanism over the United States Government.

CHAPTER I.

INTRODUCTORY.

THE sentiment of the homeless one that "there is no place like home," is not only significant of the fact that we generally appreciate what we are deprived of, but that there is a disposition to be attached to the place of our nativity. Perhaps Phrenologists will claim that this is proven by the bump on the human skull they call "inhabitativeness;" and while it is common for people to emigrate in order to find a better country, those who have this organ largely developed had better not remove from the place of their nativity, or their experience may be like others who, after emigrating to another country, becoming discontented, have made their way back to their old neighborhood to remain the rest of their days. This peculiar disposition is developed in the history of the Jews, who, in their captivity in a strange land, "wept when they remembered Zion," saying, "If I forget thee, O, Jerusalem, let my right-hand forget her cunning;" and doubtless they never will be satisfied until, according to their faith, they shall return to their own Jerusalem.

And this sentiment is echoed from every country where they sing in the praises of their native land. In our own country it is "Hail Columbia;" "Yankee Doodle," in the North, and "Dixie," in the South, while in North Carolina it is, "Hurrah for the Old North State forever."

As this trait is so general, it is hard to find one who will write impartial history, and not be prejudiced in favor of his own, or against another section. Even if people live in the poorest or meanest locality, they will suffer no disparagement of it, and will not suffer the truth to be told about it. Perhaps many will remember the sketches by "Porte Crayon," in Harper's Magazine, years ago, entitled "N. Carolina Illustrated," and how the press of the State criticized them; yet his sketches were generally drawn from real life, though he generally gave the ludicrous side of it. Those who have traveled in Eastern N. Carolina will recognize the naturalness of the scene of "Our Sal," represented by a bare-footed maiden, just returned from bringing home the cows, riding bareback on a mule, and at the door of a piny-woods cabin, while near by is the well with the sweep, and the cypress-knee bucket, and in the rear a few slim fodder stacks.

The tourists who travel over N. Carolina on the great thoroughfares, viewing the best residences, seeing and conversing with a few of the most prominent citizens, and visiting the watering places, get only a one-sided view of the social life of the people. So it is that much of history will be one-sided. And although orators, North and South, may descant on fraternity, union, &c., doubtless sectionalism will continue to exist more or less until the millenium. In this connection I will state that the people in the Western section of the State regard the Albemarle region as a very sickly region; but let one travel over the lowlands there, and he will hardly be able to find the sickly place. And he will find some that will rather resent the imputation that they have chills and fever down there. Perhaps some may ask if the writer is an exception to the rule laid down above, and may inquire, "where were you born, Sir?" Well, of course, I was born somewhere, and though present on the occasion, could not help being born just where I was, and if questioned closely might be found to sympathize with the darkey away down South, as he sings, "O, carry me back to Old Virginny." But after all, my purpose is to

"Seize upon truth where'er 'tis found,
On Christian or on heathen ground."

ignoring sectionalism and sectarianism, and inviting one and all of my readers to bring every moral sentiment advanced to the test of the scriptures, by which all character and conduct is to be measured.

CHAPTER II.

Retrospection—Emigration to North Carolina—Early Experiences—Schools and School Masters, &c.

FROM my introductory it will be understood that I did not first see the light in North Carolina. I came here in my boyhood, and have spent most of my life here. Although more than half a century has passed, my recollection is vivid of my starting from Old Virginia, which was my first experience in traveling alone, the journey being by stage coach to the little village of Danville, then a horseback ride to Guilford county, stopping for the night at a country inn, the same house now standing in the midst of Reidsville.

Considering the advancement made here during the half-century, in education, &c., the question may arise as to whether there has been a corresponding advancement in the moral and religious life of the people. This is doubtful, and if people are better now than in the former days, it is certain that they have not as much confidence in the integrity of each other, as in former days. Perhaps there may be a larger per centage of the population that are members of some church, but doubtless there is more of the world in the church now than any of us ever knew before, and perhaps it is harder to enforce church disipline; and it seems that the record of to-day shows more corruption in politics, financial affairs, and social life than in the past; and it is fearful to think of the record of crime in our State during a single year, while it is no better, but worse, in some other States. In the good old days of revival and camp meetings, people generally began a religious life by getting down on their knees and praying for mercy, but now it is rather the style to walk up and give the preacher the hand, and so be counted as a convert. Perhaps it may be said that old styles have changed, but the style of repentance and faith was not intended to change, and the handshaking may fail to shake up people as they have need to be shaken. I am not much of an optimist, my experience and knowledge of people forbidding it; I simply believe those to be good who practice goodness, which is in agreement with the scriptural declaration, that "he that doeth righteousness is righteous."

On reaching North Carolina, one novel sight to me was a Quaker, and it was not long before I had an opportunity of attending one of their silent meetings. While they all sat with bowed heads, the men with their hats on, not one looking back to see others who were coming in, I was a little frisky on my seat, and peeping around to see what could be seen, I caused the "Spirit" to move one old Elder to get up and reproved "some young people who didn't behave very well." But the old style Quaker seems to be passing away, and giving place to a class who have gotten out of the old ruts, many of them having dropped the old garb, and their silent meetings changed into the exercises of singing, exhortation, &c.; and I learn that at their Yearly Meeting last year, a move was made to introduce vocal and instrumental music into their N. C. College.

Another new thing to me was a woman in the pulpit, which now is not so much of a novelty. And she is still moving towards the front, and perhaps will "get there" before long. In fact she seems to be occupying the position assigned her by a popular speaker not long ago, that although the man is the head, "the woman is the *neck* that turns the head about."

Since forty years ago many changes have taken place in the habits and social life of the people. The Negro trader was a noted character in those days. Richmond, Va., was the great slave market, and after gathering a drove of slaves, men, women and children, the trader would pass along with his caravan the great highway leading South, the Danville and Salisbury road, the able-bodied slaves being on foot, and while the future was so dark to them, they would often raise their voices in song as they passed along. But the sword came upon our land, and slavery has become a thing of the past, and the memory of those past scenes seems like a dream. How strange it was that the love of gain so blinded the minds of men, that they would undertake to establish, by the Scriptures, the moral right to buy and sell another man, whom God had made a moral agent, and responsible to him.

And what a change has taken place in schools, and the methods of teaching. The schools in those days were known as "loud schools," the scholars being required to repeat their lessons aloud while memorizing them; and when so engaged there would be a perfect babel-jargon of voices. The process of learning to read and write was a slow one, the scholar being required to spell through the book several times, then go through a course of easy reading, and then begin the process of writing, by first making straight marks and "pot hooks." The goose-quill pen was the only one in use then, which would be a curiosity in the school of to-day, though not entirely obsolete. Perhaps I might be regarded as a specimen of the "old fogy," when I state that the whole manuscript of this book was written with a quill pen, of my own make, which suited my purpose better than a steel pen.

As to school discipline, the mildest form was the "dunce block;" but the switch was regarded as indispensible, and was doubtless in many cases a better persuader than "moral suasion," though some school reformers advocate "moral suasion" only; but it is doubtful if they are any wiser than Solomon, who, in the book of Proverbs, recommends "the rod" as well as reproof, as a means of correction.

To give an idea of some of the schools of those past years, I remember that on one occasion a man applied for the position of teacher of a free school, when it was necessary to have a certificate of "good moral character," but he being of rather dissipated habits, there was some difficulty in his case; but finally he found one who gave him a certificate of "good moral character during school hours;" so he was employed, and a notice was put up for the school to commence, as follows:

"Notis. The free Scule in district no——will commence on the——day of—— 184—, and we the comity certify that we have implowed—— to tech sade Scule."——————— ⎫
——————— ⎬ Comity.
——————— ⎭

I spent the winter of 1842 in one of the counties west of the Blue Ridge, and concluded to make up a little school, which was my first attempt in that line. In that day, a man was regarded as competent to teach school, if he could "read, write and cipher." I met with a young man in the neighborhood who aspired to teach also, and he put me through a kind of examination, giving me some of his hard questions, his hardest being a sum in the Double Rule of Three, which I readily worked, and so my reputation was established. I commenced teaching, having scholars ranging from the little tow-headed urchin to the grown up boy and girl. I had the old-style rules to govern the school, but exercised but little moral influence over it, for the reason that I was not moral enough to do so.

I will not undertake to give an account of the morals prevailing there at that time, but will note a few incidents, by way of illustration. A little while after the school had gotten under way, among the day scholars there came a full grown young woman who, after school was dismissed, wished me to go home with her, which I was too bashful to do, but promised to go the next evening, which I did, and found that her whole object in coming to school that one day, was to get me to go to her home and write a *love-letter* for her to her sweetheart, who was a rowdy fellow, and who was in jail at that time.

I wrote the letter as she dictated it, and it certainly was a most gushing affair.

As the Christmas holidays began to draw near, it was talked around that the usual custom of "turning out" the school master was to be carried out, and when the crisis came I gave in and accepted the terms decided on, which was a treat of half a gallon of brandy for an eggnog, as my views on the liquor question were not so decided as in after years. But the eggnog was rather a failure as the eggs, could not be had; but the brandy and the milk were put into a kettle, and put on the fire, and a kind of a stew was made that couldn't exactly be named, and it was thus dealt out to the crowd. During the school I spent several nights visiting the patrons of the school, the entertainment around the roaring log fire being that of eating chestnuts and listening to the girls sing the old time love songs.

During my sojourn there I heard no preaching but that of the Hard Shell Baptists, and not much of that. The first sermon I heard at any church there made an *impression*. The regular preacher failed to appear, and an old neighborhood preacher was put in as a substitute. It was in the month of December, I think, and the portly old fellow arose, and taking off his jeans coat, and hanging it up in the pulpit behind him, and, making some apologies, said, "I will now try to preach to you, notwithstanding my *illability*, and no countness," and then he went at it like killing snakes.

Before leaving that section of country, I had another glimpse of social life, at a marriage which came off not far away. On the evening of the marriage, among the company that gathered, was a Hard Shell preacher, who was to be master of ceremonies, and while the preliminaries were being arranged, some one gave the signal that a little private entertainment was to be had, a little way down in the woods, and I followed the crowd, the parson being among them, and soon a jug of liquor was hauled out from under a log and was passed around, the preacher taking a hand also, as if he was used to it.

The wedding itself was not a very elaborate affair, the parents of the bride living in a one-room log house, one corner of which served for the "bridal chamber," and another for the sleeping apartment of the parents of the bride, while guests spent the night around the fireside in a kind of frolic, being led by a noted singer of love songs. Some of the incidents of the evening are rather too ludicrous to record. Some years afterward I met Col. G., a member of the legislature from that place, and I had it from his own mouth that there were living in that section two married couples, who were mutually dissatisfied with each other, not finding their affinities, as some put it, and that the two men actually "swapped wives," one giving the other "two barrels of corn to boot."

In those days it was customary for the women to attend public gatherings, such as elections, musters, and even hangings. It didn't take as much to "rig up" a girl then as it does now. It required no "Saratoga trunk" to contain her wardrobe; perhaps a calico dress, and shoes for a rarity, and jewelry, consisting, perhaps, of a single brass ring; and the matter of putting on the paint was simple and inexpensive. Having prepared the material beforehand, consisting of cotton rags soaked in pokeberry juice and dried, when needed it would simply be necessary to moisten a little and apply it to the cheeks. Now about noon at such gatherings a young fellow would take his "best girl" up to a cart where cakes and cider were to be had, and treat her, and soon, with a large cake of gingerbread and a mug of cider, she would seem to enjoy the occasion finely. Then would come on the dance. Having selected a suitable place in the grove, and about a fifth rate fiddler taking his stand, some would enter the contest for the championship, two dancers at a time, competing one with the other, while near by a squad of white and colored mixed, would engage in playing marbles. Later on, the fisticuffs would be in order, and under such circumstances, we may suppose, somebody "struck Billy Patterson."

CHAPTER III.

The Darkey as I have seen him in North Carolina—His ruling traits, and his religious character—Some noted ones.

AN anonymous writer, about the time of the civil war, took the position that the negro does not belong to Adam's race, and that he went into the ark with Noah as an animal, &c. This ridiculous theory is based on the supposition that God created another race of human beings besides Adam and Eve, and to support such an idea, it is claimed that, according to the Bible, at the time that Cain killed Abel there were only Adam and Eve, and Cain and Abel, in the world, and that on reaching the land of Nod Cain saw, or found, his wife, which is a palpable blunder. The language of scripture in this connection implies that Cain carried his wife with him to the land of Nod, and of course she must have been a daughter of Adam. Bible history says, "Two of the children of Adam and Eve are alone mentioned—Cain and Abel. Not that there were no others, but that the progress of scripture history is connected with these two. For the Bible does not profess to give a detailed history of the world, nor even a complete biography of those persons whom it introduces. Its object is to set before us a history of the Kingdom of God, and it only describes such persons and events as are necessary for that purpose." The record is that after Cain and Abel were grown up, "in process of time," they went down to the field, when Cain killed his brother. It might have been forty years, a sufficient time for Adam to have had a number of grown-up daughters. Besides this, as a proof that the negro is of Adam's race, he is by nature, in moral character, depraved, like the white race, and simply commits the same kind of sins they are guilty of.

While the Anglo Saxon race has been perplexed in regard to the origin of the negro, he himself seems but little concerned about it. It is related that soon after the war a North Carolina preacher of rather peculiar mental caliber wrote out a lecture on the origin of the negro for publication, but first wished to deliver it in his own vicinity, in order to get the opinion of his friends in regard to it, and made an appointment accordingly. In the afternoon before the night of the lecture he went into his cotton field, where the following dialogue is said to have taken place between him and one of his negro tenants. "Well, Sam, are you going to the lecture tonight?" "What lecture, sir?" "My lecture, I am going to deliver tonight." "I dunno, sir; what's it about?" "It's on the negro, showing where he came from." "Well, I dunno as I keer so much 'bout where I cum from, but I'd like to know sumthin 'bout whar I'm gwine to, sir."

Very recently a noted newspaper correspondent wrote an article in regard to the negro race in the South, implying that they had a natural propensity to theft; and his article was replied to by an African bishop, who made a telling remark in that connection. He said, "A white man will steal more at one grab than a darkey will in forty years." After all, the negro race seems to be the most religious of any in the world, and he falls into the exercises of singing and praying, &c., throwing himself into it with all the enthusiasm that he did in the old time corn songs and the dance. A prominent Methodist D. D., who traveled in the South on a tour of observation, turning his attention particularly to the colored race, after much observation said, "It seems to me that the negro has taken to religion as a matter of amusement, in place of his former employment of banjo playing, singing and dancing."

Here I will say, from my own observation, that he accepts of the Christian faith without questioning it, and in all my travels I never remember to have met with a deistical or infidel negro. The surroundings of the race, when the war was over, wre favorable for the cultivation of superstition and fanaticism; and so the trance was not uncommon among them. During their religious exercises they would fall prostrate, and remain for hours, apparently in an unconscious state, and on recovering from it would tell most wonderful tales about going to heaven, and hell, and what they saw there. Some of those people, in reporting their trip to heaven and what they saw there, don't exactly agree with the Bible account of that heavenly country, and the nature of celestial things. It is reported that one fellow after coming out of his trance, and telling of what he saw in heaven, said he "saw a great big clock settin up in de corner," and a woman standing by said, "dats de trufe, for I seed it myself when I was dar."

It was related that another woman, after her trance, and telling of her trip to heaven, said, when she reached there they "set her down to supper;" and telling about the cake that was on the table, said, "Old Mistiss used to make mighty good cake, but it wasen't nothin at all to de cake Massa Jesus give me; and I eat cake, and I eat cake, and 'twas so good I was 'bliged to take a piece and slip it in my bosom." The last expression indicates "the ruling passion strong" in heaven. Again, it was related that in one of their meetings a young girl had been lying prostrate, and apparently insensible, and while a number were gathered around her, the preacher among them with the Bible in hand, she began to revive, and made an effort to rise, when the preacher, slamming the Bible down on her, said, "Lie dar till Jesus tell you ter git up."

I do not undertake to explain the phenomena of the trance, but if it was not hypocritical it might be called a kind of hallucination; or was it an epidemic? It was not more extraordinary than what was called "the jerks," which prevailed in this country, among the Methodists, many years ago, and which appeared to be a contagious thing, seizing both saint and sinner.

One thing I am satisfied of, that all such physical demonstrations in religion do not indicate any advanced state of morals or spirituality. One thing I will say in this connection, that the colored race are unsurpassed in congregational singing. They don't produce any scientific music, or come up to the standard of fashionable singing, but they sing with a vim and with enthusiasm, and whatever our opinion may be in regard to their religion, let one draw near to their worshiping assembly and listen to the full chorus of voices, as in full accord it swells out upon the evening air, and if there is anything like devotion in him he will be moved in sympathy with them. And what attention they give to the preacher; and the responses they give during the sermon, such as "that's so," "yes, yes," "listen, listen;" while others sway their bodies to and fro, bowing their heads nearly to the floor, and keeping up a kind of moan, with audible expressions of "yes, Lord," &c.

One fact may be here stated, that perhaps none will deny, that the colored church members give more in support of their religion, in proportion to their means, than the whites do. They have their church entertainments, festivals, &c., in order to raise money for church purposes. I will give a novel method which they put in practice in our town the past season. They appointed an entertainment to come off at their meeting house, putting the price of admittance at ten cents. The entertainment consisted of a live rabbit being turned loose in the house, after closing the doors, one dollar being the prize offered to the one who should catch it; and we may imagine what a scramble there was after it, by the darkies of that congregation.

I had a very good opportunity of seeing the darkey, as he is in North Carolina, while canvassing in the eastern counties of the State, in the work of the American Bible Society, and I can say that, with the exception of a few of the meanest specimens I found about Weldon and Halifax, I generally found them kind and respectful to the stranger. Sometimes I would come across one who wished to know my name, and instead of using the old stereotype phrase of "what might your name be?" he would ask, "what is your entitlement, sir?"

I met with one in Hertford county whose memory I wish to perpetuate, as a bright example of hospitality. It was in the month of June, and about noon that I found myself in a settlement of well-to-do colored people, and halting near a respectable looking dwelling, had called and gotten some horse feed and returned to my buggy. I had given out the idea of getting any dinner, as there was no white settler near. By this time the man of the house had returned from the field, and came out to me, whom I found to be a pleasant looking, copper colored man, and he insisted on carrying my horse into his lot to feed him; and having done so, he invited me into his house. By this time dinner was on hand, and what I called a good dinner, too, of bacon and cabbage, good corn pone. milk, &c. I was invited to partake of it; but here a question arose. Of course, I could not expect a whole family to abandon their own table to be monopolized by a single stranger, whose skin was not much whiter than theirs. Then came the query, "are you going to sit down and eat with the darkies?" But the question was settled by my *empty stomach* which refused to recognize the color line; and I sat down and enjoyed that dinner. After dinner, on fixing up to start, my host refused to have anything for what he had done for me. On asking him his name, he said it was Wright Holloman. Yes, said I, that's your name; it's not Wrong Holloman at all; and I took leave of him with pleasant thoughts. I met with him afterward and learned that he was a member of the Baptist church, and doubtless his name was written in heaven.

Some of the politest darkies I ever knew were found in the region of the Albemarle Sound, whose masters had tried to teach them good manners. Sometimes I have passed squads of them working in the cotton field, by the road-side, and they would take off their hats, making a bow, and ask, "how do you do to-day, sir?" A friend of mine who lived down in that region had a young fellow as black as a mink, who will serve as a good example. He was a house servant, and his master's house was the preacher's home when he was in the vicinity. The boy having waited on the preacher faithfully for some time, Christmas morning found him there, and thinking it a proper time to make the servant a little present, when he came into his room he took out a small coin and offered it to him, but he, stepping back, spreading out his hands, and making a low bow said, "No, I thank you, sir, I can't take it; not at all, sir; I can't take money from a preacher, sir; wish I had something to give you, sir." There was one very notable character among the colored race here, whom I had the opportunity of being particularly acquainted with. He was peculiar and stood almost alone among his fellows; in that he lived to be an old man, and died unmarried. Who can remember another old bachelor negro? He was known as "Uncle Lige," was a full-blooded African, and lived and died in Guilford county. He was most remarkable as a religious character. Before the war he was a slave of Rev. W. J. Ogburn, who in his earlier years had taught him to read. He was a member of the church at Flat Rock, and after the war did not leave it to join any of the colored church organizations. He was a habitual Bible reader, and was deep in religious experience, and was most gifted and powerful in prayer. On occasions of religious services in the church he would occasionally be called upon to make public prayer, and a prominent minister, who was pastor of that church, said that "Uncle Lige" was one of the ablest men in prayer he ever knew, white or colored.

He was by no means popular with the neighboring darkies, for he would not engage in their frolics or spend the Sabbath in idleness or in violation of the holy day, but he was esteemed by the best class of white people, and often spent the Sabbath in visiting them, and engaging in religious conversation. He did not offer to sermonize or make public addresses, or to gather a congregation of white or colored, but acted rather as a neighborhood missionary, attending prayer meetings and seeking religious conversation with individuals, and especially with young men; and he had his converts among them. The first religious services I ever engaged in I was prompted to it by "Uncle Lige," and several other ministers, now living, professed religion under his influence.

But certainly the most noted and truly great, full-blooded African ever born in North Carolina has recently died. This was Rev. J. C. Price, D. D., President of Livingstone College for the colored race, at Salisbury. At the close of the civil war he was a lad of some eight or ten years. He attended the Shaw University at Raleigh, and professed religion while a student there, and continuing his education was ordained to the ministry of the M. E. Zion Church. His extraordinary gifts being recognized, he was elected to their General Conference and also sent as a delegate to the Ecumenical Council in London in 1881, and there his efforts laid the foundation for Livingstone College. Few persons of any race ever rose to a higher eminence in so short a time, for he was under forty years of age when he died.

The first and only time I ever saw J. C. Price was during the Prohibition campaign in N. C. in 1881, when he made an address in the court-house at Louisburg. I had never heard of such a man as Price, and going in I found him addressing a small audience. There he stood, as black as a crow, in contrast with the white wall behind him, pouring out words of eloquence and logic. My first impression was that he was employed by the prohibitionists, and was simply letting off a borrowed and memorized speech; but that idea was wide of the mark, and I found out afterward that he was in his native element. One fact in his history stamps him as a great man in the truest sense. While he was struggling with obstacles, in his efforts to establish an institution of learning for the benefit of his race, and needed money, the President of the United States tendered him an office of honor and profit; but he declined it, simply saying, "I think I can do more good at Salisbury." Where is the man of any color, in North Carolina, who would, under the same circumstances, have made such a self-denying sacrifice?

CHAPTER IV.

Preachers and preaching—Some preachers of a generation ago—Funeral preaching—Anecdotes of preachers—Self conceit.

WHILE the Episcopalians and Presbyterians in the past required a classical education, in order to enter the ministry, some of the other leading denominations of the State were on the other extreme, and admitted men to preach who were unable to read and pronounce correctly the words in the common English Bible. But much advancement has been made in ministerial education in later years. I once heard a regular camp meeting preacher say that Zaccheus "clim up into the sycamore tree, and the Lord saw him and told him to came down." And another preacher opened his prayer in the following language: "O thou sweet Songster of Israel;" and the same preacher, on a funeral occasion, uttered, perhaps, the queerest sentence a preacher ever did. He said, "we have met on this occasion to pour out the balance of the milk of human kindness over the remains of a departed brother."

I will state here that a funeral in N. Carolina does not necessarily mean a burial. It has been, and is now the custom, to have a discourse in memory of the deceased delivered, in numbers of cases, several years after the burial. Years ago in the mountain region I attended the preaching of a whole family's funeral, some of whom had been buried about fourteen years. This custom results in much inconvenience, as the favorite preacher chosen for the occasion is often not within reach, and the services, when they take place interfere with other arrangements, many times. What a sight it is to see a widower with crape on his hat, mourning for his deceased wife, and trying to make arrangements for her funeral, while his arrangements are already made to marry another wife, and, being disappointed about the funeral, marries first and afterward carries his new wife to the funeral of the other. Query: can any example be found in the scriptures or the early church, of a modern funeral, or the putting on of black, for such an occasion? And ought there not to be a reformation in these things, especially in that of the fashionable funerals in the cities, which are such a burden on families of limited means, who try toi mitate the rich?

As to the sermons of the class of preachers referred to above, of course there is not much connection between the text and the sermon. On one occasion one of these preachers discoursed at a camp meeting, and not being present, I asked a ministerial friend how he preached, and he replied; "he had three grand divisions of his subject; first, he took his text, secondly, he went away from it, and thirdly, he never came back to it any more."

I believe the poorest thing to be called a sermon I ever did hear, was just after the surrender, up in the mountains, from a man who had been a refugee during the war, and had lately returned to his home. He read for his text 1 John 4:19. His firstly was a description of the state of things before the war came on, "when we were permitted to sit under our own vine and fig tree, and worship God according to the dictates of our own consciences," &c., and he concluded his firstly with his text, Therefore, &c. Then, "secondly, this cruel war came on, ah, and fathers, sons, and brothers had to part from loved ones and go to the field of battle, ah, and the cannon balls a flyin and the bomb shells a burstin, ah, and what a time of sufferin it was, ah, Therefore, &c." "Thirdly; this cruel war is over at last, ah, and peace prevails in our land, and the flag of the Union waves over our country, ah, and we are permitted to return to our homes, and meet here tonight, and worship together as friends and neighbors, ah. Therefore, &c." If the preacher gave a single idea on his text besides what is noted here, I would like for the ministerial brother who was present with me on that occasion to speak out and say what it was.

Some preachers seem to take a pride in selecting strange and quaint texts to discourse from, which they undertake to spiritualize and make application of. A case was given me some years ago, of a preacher who took for his text the words found in Judges 7:20, "Break your pitchers," and he compared the hidden lights in the pitchers of Gideon's men, to the obscured lights of professing Christians; and he went on to show that one had the pitcher of this thing, and another the pitcher of that; and he specified one class as having the pitcher of covetousness and stinginess, so that they would not come up to their duty in giving, &c.; and the preacher wound up by an exhortation to "break their pitchers," when a colored brother arose, and advanced to the table in front of the pulpit, and laying down a nickel he said, "Here I breaks my pitcher now." This was making a practical application of the subject.

Perhaps the surroundings of the preacher have a tendency to encourage spiritual pride. Every grade of preachers have their admirers, who will flatter them to their faces, while those who criticise them adversely do so generally behind their backs, so that they cannot know what the average opinion of their qualifications really is. Besides this, perhaps the average hearer admires that kind of preaching which is on the pathetic order, rather than that which searches the conscience. How often it is that after a preacher has delivered what is simply an exhortation, some good brother will approach him, saying, "That's one of the best sermons I ever heard." This is well calculated to tempt a young preacher to think "more highly of himself than he ought to think," and if he is inclined to egotism we may look for a pretty well developed case of what the old preachers used to call "the big head." Sometimes preachers of age and experience manifest this weakness. I have a case in mind now. Years ago a young man, not a professing Christian, attended a camp meeting, where a preacher of ability had preached, after which a number of persons were among the seekers. The young man told me that shortly afterward he met with that preacher, and the conversation turned on the camp meeting, and when he told him that he was present and heard his sermon, the preacher said, "Well, didn't I slay 'em that evening?" The old nursery rhyme may very properly come in here:

>Who killed Cock Robin?
>I, said the sparrow.
>With my bow and arrow,
>I killed Cock Robin.

But this kind of preachers sometimes meet with rebuffs. It is told that on one occasion a certain brother, a matter of fact kind of a man, went to hear a preacher, and after the services were over, as they rode off together, the preacher was vain enough to ask him what he thought of his sermon, and his reply was, "Well, I think perhaps I have heard better sermons than that in my life, and may be I have heard worse, but really I can't remember where it was."

Some years ago several Conference preachers and delegates stopped for the night at a roadside un, kept by a preacher who was illiterate, with a plenty of self-conceit, and after supper he came into the room where his guests were, and laying his family Bible on the table, and opening it, said, "Now, gentlemen, if there is any passage in that book you want explained, just let me know, and I'll explain it to you." None made any reply until an old minister of intelligence spoke, and, addressing himself to the little company, asked if they knew where the passage occurs in the Bible saying of a certain character, that he "is wiser in his own eyes than seven men that can render a reason?" The application was easy to make.

Years ago my recommendation for the cure of self conceit was, a few weeks sojourn with Bro. J. S, N., of the Albemarle region. While he was ready to encourage young preachers, he was no flatterer of them. He was no harsh critic, though intelligent and well informed. He would put hard questions in order to draw the preacher out, and sometimes assume an opposite position in order to test his powers of argument. Sometimes he would refer to a sermon just delivered, saying, "well, brother, you told us so and so to-day in your sermon, and I would like for you to prove it."

I remember well how he used to take me through, while I was stationed in his vicinity.

On one occasion, after delivering a discourse on the parable of the rich man and Lazarus, the following colloquy took place between us. "Well, brother, you told us to-day that there was a 'great gulf fixed' between the rich man and Lazarus, and that there could be no passing, &c." "Yes, sir," I replied. "Well," said he, "if that's so I'd like to know how you are going to get the rich man to judgment?" I was silent under his scrutinizing gaze, for a while, but escaped by saying that the scripture in question does not say that there is any "fixed gulf" between the rich man and *judgment*.

But the strange thing about the self conceited man is that he is often quite popular. One character in the scriptures is represented as "giving out that himself was some great one," and they "all gave heed to him." And that is about the way it is now, and many well disposed people will take a pompous and self asserting man for what he assumes to be.

A number of persons in recent years have turned up in N. Carolina, who professed to be preachers, but were real impostors, and might have been detected with very little trouble, but many suffered themselves imposed upon by them. I remember that only a few years ago two young men of good address, and well dressed, appeared in Alamance Co. as teachers of vocal music, hailing, as they said, from Atlanta, Ga. They had their head quarters at one of the cotton mills on Haw River, and after being associated with the preachers in their meetings, one of them was licensed to preach. After awhile he turned his attention to a daughter of his landlady, who was a widow, and where there was a little money, and before long he married the daughter and carried her away with him to Texas. He persuaded the mother also to follow him, and after getting in his posession what money she had, and spending it in dissipation, she and her family were gotten back to her former home in N. Carolina, at least "wiser if not better" than they were before. In the mean time the impostor was prosecuted for bigamy and sentenced to nine years in the penitentiary.

Some cases have also occurred here, of ministers well known and of fair standing, who have come to grief. And these good souls, how they are affected when their favorite preacher falls! But this is all wrong. We should never fix our faith on any human being in such a way as that their fall would damage us spiritually. But our motto should be:

"On Christ, the solid Rock, I stand;"
"All other ground is sinking sand."

No, our faith should never be dependent on any human character, but be based upon the Word of God.

But it must not be understood that all the self conceit is confined to the ranks of the preachers, for the same class of people perhaps are to be found in every church. They seem to know exactly how to advise the preacher, and can tell him what and what not to preach; in fact, they seem fully competent to run the church, and the preacher too, and perhaps sometimes do run him somewhere else.

Sometime since I was rather startled on reading an article on the self conceited man, which I think is positively the severest thing of the kind ever put into print, and will give it here that the reader may judge for himself.

"GRADE BELOW THE FOOL.—It has been generally thought that the fool is the lowest type of man. He creates the fewest expectations. In worthlessness there is nothing beyond a fool. Such is the universal verdict concerning the fool. And this verdict we have always accepted as a finality, and acted upon it, in our dealings with mankind. Have we been correct in this? Let the Bible answer. It comes to us as a surprise, for it clashes with the universal verdict. It asserts that the fool is not the ultimatum of the lower grades of humanity. He is not the most hopeless creature at large in society. There is one grade below him. There is a hopelessness that is more hopeless than his. There is a type of man that is more barren, and unworkable, and unpromising. The self conceited man is a lower type. 'Seest thou a man wise in his own conceit? There is more hope of a fool than of him.' This is severe on self conceit. It is as severe as it is possible to be. It is positively startling. It is startling, because self conceit is a ruling passion with every tenth man we meet. Is every tenth man worse than a fool?"

From our reference to some preachers of past years it will be inferred that the standard of ministerial qualification was low; but as low as it was, it was equal to the standard of ministerial support. Just to think of a preacher giving his whole time to the service of churches for a year, and receiving less than one hundred dollars salary! In those days a preacher had served a field of labor where he had received a very meager support, and about the close of the year, after preaching his farewell sermon, he called on a close-fisted old brother to lead in prayer, who prayed that the preacher might "have souls for his hire." After services were over the preacher put to him the following question: "Brother, can a man live on souls? Can a man eat souls?" The Presbyterians in N. Carolina have adopted an honest rule in regard to ministerial support. They do not allow any church to have a new pastor while they are delinquent in paying their former pastor what they promised him. And why should not custom and public sentiment require that the same rule be applied in regard to the salary promised a preacher, as it is in the case of every other employee who renders service for specified wages?

CHAPTER V.

Illiteracy—The Bible, and mistakes about what is in it.—A remarkable Bible reader—Home-made Scripture—Misquotations, and perversions of the word.

ALTHOUGH N. Carolina has had for years a State University, and free schools have been in operation for a generation or more, yet there is a large number of grown up men and women in every section of the State who are unable to read. I had a fair opportunity of getting the facts in the case in visiting from house to house for a number of years in the work of the American Bible Society; and, what was most remarkable, the largest per centage of families found destitute of the Bible was found in the territory bordering on the Capital of the State, while the smallest per centage was found on the islands of Roanoke and Hatteras. In my canvass I could not tell how many grown up people asked me what kind of Bibles I had, and whether they were Baptist or Methodist Bibles; and one well to do farmer was particular to tell me that a Primitive Bible was the kind he wanted, meaning a Hard Shell one. During a number of years past the Bible canvass showed about one-fourth of the families destitute of the Scriptures. In some families I found Bibles dated 1829, and some a little later, which were in a good state of preservation, showing that they had been but little used except for recording the ages, or stropping the razor on Sunday morning.

Since the Revised version of the Bible has been gotten out, much prejudice exists against it; not because it is not as perfect a version as the King James Bible, but on account of a natural prejudice in favor of what is old. They say the old Bible was sufficient to guide our fathers in the way to heaven, and "The old time religion is good enough for me." On one occasion I called on a family who had no Bible, but the man said he wouldn't have anything to do with the new fashion Bibles, and after explaining to him that the Bible Society did not print the new version, and thinking I had gotten him about right to buy a Bible, his wife glanced at the title page of one, and seeing the words, "diligently compared and revised," I couldn't get them to have anything more to do with it, and left them, thoroughly disgusted with such ignorance.

In contrast with those who neglect Bible reading, I will mention one who was designated as a noted Bible reader, and who lies now in the cemetery at Fair Grove Church, in Rockingham Co., having lived and died a member of that church. On the marble slab is inscribed the name of "Elijah Chilcutt," and the statement following that at the time of his death he "was engaged in reading the Bible through for the one hundred and twenty-second time." While the Bible is the standard of truth, people are inclined to interpret it to make it fit their own creed or belief, hence there are so many errors as to what it does teach. During the civil war some had their scripture for believing that the South would prevail, and quoted the prophet's words; "I will drive back the Northern army," while one man, a Union man, believed the South would not prevail, and also quoted the words of the prophet; "Say ye not a Confederacy." But the cutest thing in the way of applying scripture to support political sentiment, I met with just after the surrender, while traveling in the mountains of N. C. I fell in with a man who was denouncing secession, and he referred to the Dragon mentioned in Revelation, who "drew with his tail a third part of the stars of heaven," and he said, "that's Jeff. Davis, for he drew with his secession tail (tale) a third part of the stars, or States of the Union, which was just the number of the States seceded."

There is hardly any end to the misquotations, and misapplication of scripture. And there is a good deal of what has been designated as "home-made scripture," i. e. quotations made of what is not in the Bible at all. For example, some quote "that the time will come when we shall not know the summer from the winter, but by the budding of the trees." "That Judas was a devil from the beginning." "That he that runs may read;" and that "each generation shall grow wiser and weaker." And some people have named their children Talitha Cumi, after the damsel Christ raised from the dead, thinking that was the name given her in the scriptures. And there is one popular error in a statement contained in several Bible works that the 19th chapter of 2 Kings, and the 37th chapter of Isaiah are alike, when there are over thirty discrepancies. I learned recently of a young man whose friends, on one occasion, tried to induce him to seek religion. He was an illegitimate, and he said there was no use for him to try to get religion, for the "Bible said a bastard couldn't go to heaven." This false idea is based on a misapprehension of Deut. 23rd chap. 2nd verse. All persons with any physical defect were excluded from membership in the Jewish worshipping congregation, simply as a type, to show how perfect, and holy, in a spiritual sense, we should be in order to dwell in the Kingdom above. That text in Deut. has disturbed the minds of others besides that young man. But all should bear in mind that only one class of persons are excluded from the kingdom of heaven, viz: those who persevere in impenitence and unbelief.

A few years ago I heard a prominent North Carolina man deliver a lecture, his subject being King David, in which he took the ground that David was one of the noblest characters that ever lived, eulogizing his virtues, and passing lightly over his transgressions; and some time afterward I met with the lecturer, and on the coming up of the subject of his lecture, I said to him, "Dr., you gave David a pretty good send off to-night." "Yes," he said, "the old rascal needed it, for he had Uriah killed in order to get his wife." This was rather a reflection on the sincerity of his lecture. But I called his attention to the evident blunder, and the popular mistake in regard to David's motive in having Uriah put to death. That, according to scripture narative, after David's transgression his movements had two objects in view—to cover up his sin, and to save the life of Bathsheba, who with himself was subject to the penalty of death, under the law of Moses. But after sending for Uriah to return home, and his purpose seeming to thwart David's purpose of concealment, then to save his own life, and that of the woman, he contrived the death of Uriah as the last resort, and then married Bathsheba. All this is clearly shown by attentively reading the narrative.

Sometimes people miss the sense of whole passages of scripture by not giving the evident sense of smoe word, or the right pronunciation of it. One man said the word "nigger" did not occur in the Bible, and another asserted that it did, and he could show it; and he turned to one of Paul's epistles and pointed to the name of Ni-ger, which he pronounced Nig-er. I once heard the pastor of a church preach to a large congregation, who made a most egregious blunder in construing his text, which was the words of the Apostle, "without controversy great is the mystery of godliness." He made the Apostle to mean that without entering into controversy, godliness is a great mystery, but by controversy it was all made plain; and then he followed out his idea by controverting the doctrines of other denominations who disagreed with him:

There is a disposition prevalent in the world to misinterpret and pervert the language of the scriptures, in order to support false doctrine, and to sanction wrong doing. While the word of God is to be used by Christians as the "Sword of the Spirit," the devil knows that the Bible contains that sword, and it is an old trick of his to misquote and pervert it. In tempting Christ, he tried to mislead him by quoting, "It is written, &c." And his servants follow his example in this, and so every heretical and false teacher quotes the scriptures in propagating his doctrine. And the Apostle Paul says it is "no marvel, for Satan himself is transformed into an Angel of Light." And habitual old sinners, in palliating their bad conduct, will refer to the example of such Bible characters as Noah and David, without any intention of following the example of the old patriarchs in their deep repentance for their transgressions. And old topers will take consolation from the fact that Paul advised Timothy to "take a little wine," as medicine or corrective of his ailments. And those who wish to engage in the dissipation of the ball room can find that little, disconnected scrap of scripture, "a time to dance."

Again, it is common for those who are neglecting their present opportunities to encourage themselves in their procrastination, by referring to the example of the laborers, who went to the vineyard at the eleventh hour, when they themselves, perhaps, have passed into the twelfth hour of life, and by referring to the "dying thief," who perhaps never heard the voice of Christ until he was dying on the cross. I will give an incident which is much to the point. A certain minister had preached from the text, "will a man rob God?" and the question was answered in the affirmative; and here is the illustration. A man asked another, "are you a believer in the Christian religion? "O, certainly." "You are a member of some church, then, I suppose." "Member of a church? No, indeed. Why should I be a member of a church? It is quite unnecessary. The dying thief wasn't a member of a church, and he went to heaven." "But, of course, you've been baptized." "Been baptized? O, no. That's another needless ceremony. I'm as safe as the dying thief was, and he never was baptized." "But, surely, since you will not join a church or be baptized, you do something in acknowledgment of your faith. You give of your means, you help the cause in some way." "No, sir, I do nothing of the kind. The dying thief——" "Let me remark, my friend, before you go any farther, that you seem to be on pretty intimate terms with the dying thief. You seem to derive a great deal of consolation from his career; but mind you, there is one important difference between you and him. He was a *dying* thief—and you are a *living* one."

There is one perversion of a passage of scripture, which is liable to do much mischief, and to my certain knowledge, in more than one case, it has been used for the basest purpose, and to lead others into transgression. I allude to 1 Cor. 7th chapter, 36th verse. The term "his virgin" does not refer to a man's espoused wife, but to his virgin daughter, and by reading the 37th and 38th verses, any one may see that the whole question involved is that of a man giving, or not giving, his virgin daughter in marriage.

Again, many take the figurative language of the Bible in a literal sense, and so mistake the meaning. For instance, the idea is generally prevalent that at the end of the world, countless multitudes of stars will fall to the earth. The absurdity of such an idea will appear when it is remembered that the most of stars, which are distant worlds, are larger than our earth, and if one were to fall on the earth, there would be no room for another one; and the scripture term "stars of heaven" falling, often refers to the fall of civil rulers, &c. Here mark that in Gen. 37:9-10, the sun and moon and eleven stars, plainly refer to Joseph's father and mother and eleven brothers. No doubt many will remember that some years since a song was sung by some of the preachers in this section of the country, containing the words, "O, the moon it will be bleeding in that day;" the song being no doubt composed by one who believed that at the end of the world the moon will be literally turned into blood.

Sometimes scripture language may be perverted by even the want of proper punctuation of a single sentence. As an illustration it has been related that a certain preacher in quoting Rev. 12:1, made a pause after the word woman, thus making the wonder to consist, not in her being "clothed with the Sun," but the fact of a woman being in heaven. As an illustration of how even scriptural doctrine may be abused, and made a subterfuge, I will mention the idea conveyed in the talents, that "where little is given, little is required," and give an incident. I met a young man, and inquired if he had a Bible. He answered, "No, I haven't got any; I don't want any, and wouldn't read one if I had it." On inquiring of him why he wouldn't read the Bible, he said, people told him that where there was "little given, little was required;" and he didn't know much, and didn't want to know any more, for fear he would have to give an account of it. I gave him to understand that a man would have to give account of, not only what he knows, but what he dont know, and might know, but refuses to know; and that the guiltiest kind of a man is the one who dodges the opportunity to know his duty; and I left that young man with the impression that he would pass for a first-class fool.

I met another man who would answer for a sample of the same kind. On inquiring if he had a Bible, he said, "No;" he couldn't read. I told him if I was no older than he was, I would get me a spelling book, and, if I could do no better, would go around among my neighbors and get them to teach me. He replied; "I don't care nothing about education no how; it ain't no account; it jest makes a man a rascal."

CHAPTER VI.

Superstition—Belief in Witches—Conjuration—Spells, &c.—Other humbugs.

THE Apostle Paul said, on Mars Hill, "Ye men of Athens, I perceive that in all things ye are too superstitious;" and people in every age and country have been inclined to believe in the supernatural. These beliefs have been prevalent in N. Carolina, as well as elsewhere. It seems that all the witchcraft has not been confined to New England, for it is stated in one of the histories, that the second person ever executed in N. C. was a woman, who was put to death on a charge of witchcraft. And perhaps the masses here now are as ready to be humbugged as any other people, and are often made the victims of some plausible scheme, the popular newspapers of the day containing advertisements which carry in their faces the marks of falsehood and deception.

Perhaps the greatest humbug, and the most plausible one, in the book line, that has been introduced into our State is, "Bible Readings for the Home Circle," which is being sold by canvassing agents in different parts of the State. From the title, the unsuspecting people think they are getting a valuable exposition of the scriptures for family use, when it proves to be a selection of Bible readings twisted and perverted to make them fit the false ideas of the Seventh day Second Adventists, whose headquarters are at Battle Creek, Michigan; and the agents seem to be acting rather as missionaries, and wherever they go are active in talking up the Advent doctrines. While the Protestant orthodox faith prevails in N. Carolina, a number of heretical isms have been imported here, which have had proselytes more or less in several localities, among which may be named Universalists, Second Adventists, Spiritualists, and Mormons. The Mormons found a lodgment in Surry county a number of years ago, and during the past year or two, some of them have passed around in Chatham, Alamance, and Guilford, and tried to introduce their faith into several localities. Their plan has been to seek the most out-of-the-way neighborhoods, and, going two and two, to drop in upon some unsuspecting farmer about night, introducing themselves as ministers of the gospel; and if asked of what denomination, they say they belong to the "Church of Jesus Christ." Where they are entertained they generally leave a handbill containing a synopsis of their faith. While nothing should be said to discourage the exercise of hospitality towards individual strangers in need,

I will take the responsibility of saying that it is unscriptural to receive Mormon impostors or to entertain them as ministers of the gospel. See 2 Epistle of John, 10th and 11th verses. If any man is disposed to accept of the Mormon faith, which is based on the bare assertion of one Joe Smith, that an angel appeared to him, and revealed certain things to him, then he is a fit subject to be numbered as "one of the fools."

There are a number of what may be called harmless superstitions among the people, such as burning flint rocks in the fire to keep hawks from catching the chickens; that certain dreams or omens are a sure sign of so and so, that will surely come to pass, &c. But there are some other superstitions that are not so harmless. For example, some years ago I was in a community where the belief was prevalent that certain persons had the power to lay spells on others, by conjuration, and, like the Puritans of New England, who had their "Matthew Hopkins, the Witch Finder," they had their witch Doctor, to whom they went when his services were in demand. In one case it was said that a man had a mule that refused to work and took to kicking, and thinking that a "spell" had been laid upon him by some of the conjurors, he took him to the witch Doctor to get him to take it off.

On one occasion a certain preacher, in a pulpit not far off, denounced the Witch Doctor as an imposter, classing him with "Simon the Sorcerer," but it seemed as if the Witch Doctor was more popular than the preacher in that community. I cannot say how much the said Doctor received for his services, but it is a historical fact that a church not far off, that was assessed forty-five dollars for the preacher's salary, paid, at the end of the year, just one dollar and sixty-five cents. That might be pretty good territory for the gypsies to operate in.

In my travels, during a number of years past, I have several times seen a document in the possession of persons, who seemed to hold it in superstitious reverence. It claims to be "a letter written by Jesus Christ," while he was upon earth, and came to light after his resurrection and ascension. It bears plainly upon its face evidence of being a forgery. Having taken a copy of it, I will quote from it, and the reader can judge for himself. "The following letter was written by Jesus Christ, and found under a great stone, both round and large, at the foot of the cross, eighteen miles from Iconium, near a village called Mesopotamia, sixty-five years after our Savior's crucifixion, transmitted from the Holy City, by a converted Jew, faithfully translated from the original Hebrew copy, now in the possession of the Lady Cuba's family, at Mesopotamia. Upon that stone was written and engraved, 'Blessed is he that turneth me over.' All that saw it prayed to God earnestly, and desired He would make known to them the meaning of this writing, that they might not attempt, in vain, to turn it over. In the mean time there came a little child, about six years old, who turned it over, without help, to the astonishment of all who stood by; and under the stone was found a letter written by Jesus Christ, which was carried to the city of Iconium, and there published by a person belonging to the Lady Cuba, and on the letter was written the Commands of Jesus Christ, and signed by the Angel Gabriel, twenty-eight years after our Savior's crucifixion." It is not necessary to give the whole of the letter, in order that the reader may judge as to its genuiness, and I will simply give some extracts.

"LETTER OF JESUS CHRIST."

"I command you to go to church, and keep the Lord's day holy, without doing any manner of work. This was written by my own hand, spoken by my own mouth. You shall not only go to church yourselves, but also your men servants, and your maid servants, and observe my words, and learn my commandments. You shall finish your labor every Saturday, in the afternoon, by six of the clock, at which hour the preparation of the Sabbath begins. I advise you to fast five Fridays in every year, beginning with Good Friday, and to continue the four Fridays immediately following, in remembrance of the five bloody wounds I received for all mankind. You shall love one another with brotherly love, and cause them that are not baptized to come to church and hear the holy sacrament, viz: Baptism and the Lord's Supper, and be made members thereof. In so doing I will give you long life, and many blessings. And he that hath a copy of this letter, written with my own hand, and spoken with my own mouth, and keeps it, without publishing it to others, shall not prosper, but he that publishes it to others shall be blessed of me; and if he believes not this writing, and my commandments, I will send my plagues upon him, and consume both him and his children, and his cattle; and whosoever has a copy of this letter, and keep it in their houses, nothing shall harm them, neither pestilence, lightning, or thunder. You shall have no news of me, but by the Holy Spirit, till the day of judgment."

I will suggest, that to my mind, there are three reasons for believing the letter to be a forgery.

1st. That it contains no moral precept that is not contained in the recorded Gospels and Epistles of the New Testament. 2nd. That the word Good Friday, contained in it, is proof that it has been gotten up since the days of Christ and the Apostles, as no such word was recognized in New Testament times. 3rd. That the writer, since first seeing it a dozen years ago, has denounced it as a fraud and a humbug, and yet has been visited with none of the curses pronounced against those who do not believe in the letter.

Another letter of Christ has turned up, found this time by Missionaries, being in circulation in homes in lower New York. It claims to have been found originally in the Holy Sepulchre at Jerusalem, and preserved by his Holiness in a silver box. It fathers itself in the following paragraph: "I shed 38,325 drops of blood, and he who will repeat every day, for fifteen years, seven Pater Ave Glorias, to make up for the drops of blood shed, and fast five Fridays in the year, I will grant five requests of which the first shall be complete indulgence, and remission of all his sin. Second: Freedom from the sufferings of purgatory. Third: if he dies before the fifteen years expire, it shall be as though he had completed them. Fourth: it will be as if he had died shedding all his blood for the Christian faith. Fifth: I will come from heaven for such souls, and the souls of their children, to the fourth generation." It is evident that the authorship of this letter can be traced to no higher source than some Roman Catholic monk or priest; and the other letter bears the same marks.

As we are taught in the parable of the rich man and Lazarus, that God's written revelation embraces all that is necessary for us to know in regard to His will concerning us, no dependence is to be placed in any new light or revelation, outside of the scriptures, to establish any doctrine not contained in the Book; so the conclusion is that Spiritualism, Mormonism, and every other ism of like character must be false. Yet it does appear that persons do sometimes receive a kind of inspiration or presentiment, by which they are apprised of things that are taking place, or that will take place, and a number of such cases are on record.

In illustration I will give the following historical facts, which I gathered while on Pigeon river, in Haywood county, some years ago. A young woman living near by, made a visit to an aunt living over the river, which she crossed on the foot-log, which is the usual way of crossing small streams in that country, on foot; and, as usual, this log had a hand-railing to it. She went to spend the night, and to return next morning. In the morning she related a very singular dream she had during the night. She dreamed that she had started home, and after getting near the river she sat down on a large rock to rest awhile, and then started to cross on the log, and walked on, until she had gotten about half way, and where one of the hand-railings had been broken off, just where one of the little posts had been driven into an auger hole in the log, when she suddenly fell off into the stream and was drowned. On relating her dream, the family where she was visiting insisted that she should not start for home that morning, especially as there had been much rain during the night, and the stream was now a rushing torrent. But she persisted in her determination to go, and so a young man in the family went with her to see her over the river. When he returned, he related that they went on until the rock was reached, which the young woman dreamed she sat down on, and, strange to say, she took a seat on it! Then proceeding they got on the log, he taking the lead, and holding her by the hand; and they went on steadily until they reached the auger hole in the log, when she was seized with a trembling, and fell from the log into the rushing waters, pulling him in after her; and she was drowned, and he himself barely escaped drowning, to return and tell the tale. This remarkable incident I obtained while in the vicinity.

There are some things that may be regarded by many as superstitions, but which, we are bound to admit, contain some mysterious facts, which are not so easy to dispose of. Of course, many have signs and omens, which may be included under the head of "old wives' fables;" the voice of the whippoorwill, near the house, or the crowing of a rooster, with his head in a certain position, being a prophecy of some important family event. Some people have regard to the moon, being regulated by it in the planting of vegetables, &c. In regard to these things, some may be incredulous; but if the moon has such a marked effect on the tides of the ocean, why may it not have a like effect in respect to the seed, or the soil of the earth?

It is claimed that some persons have the power to remove certain bodily ailments, without applying any medicinal remedy. For instance, some profess to take away warts, by simply mumbling a few words, and rubbing their hands over the warts. And cases have been known where persons' hands that were covered with warts, were treated in that way, and the warts soon disappeared. Again, some claim the power to stop blood from a dangerous cut or wound, without any visible application. Not long ago a man, whom I regarded as reliable, related to me a case, which he said occurred during the war, and to which he was an eye witness. He said a soldier was badly wounded; an artery, or a large vein, being severed and the blood spurting out; and those having him in charge feared the man would be dead before the surgeon could reach him, when a man standing near said, "I can stop it." Another said, "You had better begin very quickly, then." The other said, after a few moments of silence, "I have done what I aim to do." Then in a few moments the flow of blood was plainly decreasing, and in a little while more it ceased to flow, the wound was bound up, and the man recovered. This is the account given by my informant, which I do not undertake to explain. I will add, however, that I learn that the main formula used in this blood-stopping process consists of the repeating of a passage of Scripture, found in Ezekiel 16th chapter and 6th verse.

CHAPTER VII.

Religious denominations in N. C.—Camp Meetings—Some differences between Eastern and Western N. Carolina—Anecdotes of preachers.

PERHAPS the people of N. Carolina are as religious as they are in any other section of our country, at least there are as many religious denominations as in any other territory of the same extent. They embrace five organizations of Methodists, three of Baptists, three of Presbyterians, two of Lutherans, one of German Reformed. one of Episcopalians, one of Disciples or Campbellites, one of the Christian or O'Kelly branch, one of Friends or Quakers, one of Moravians; and, then, there are a few Tunker or Dunkards, Universalists, and Second Adventists, who claim to be Protestants, but are not regarded as orthodox. Besides these, there are within the bounds of the State a few thousands of Roman Catholics, embracing a bishop and fifteen priests, with twenty-two churches, a number of chapels, a college, and a seminary, and more than a dozen other schools. These are ruled by a foreign pope, who claims to occupy the chair of St. Peter, and claims supreme jurisdiction over all the territory of earth; thus rivaling the devil, who, in the presence of Christ, claimed "all the kingdoms of the world." But my purpose is to give more than a passing notice to Romanism; and I have decided to add a chapter or more to this volume, showing from the scriptures that the papacy is the great Anti Christ.

I will mention here that a colony of Waldenses have recently settled in Burke county, which will add another Protestant denomination to the population of our State. And there is a little band or sect, claiming to be "no sect," up in the mountain region, who are known as "come outers." They hold that all of the different sects have departed from primitive Christianity, and their idea is, that if any one is a member of any of the denominational churches, let them "come out" of that, and join with them, and make a true Bible church. What a rediculous pretension that is; for while separating themselves from all other sects, they make of themselves another sect, and the name of their sect is "no sect." Like all others who profess to discard all creeds, and take the Bible for their guide, they want everybody to take their interpretation of it for a guide, so there can be no unity of sentiment on such a basis, and the question of unity of faith remains just as it was, while each individual claims the right of private judgment, in the interpretation of the sciptures.

In years gone by it was not uncommon to have debates, when two denominational champions would meet, and discuss the issues betwwen them, the contest lasting sometimes several days, and at the close, the friends of each would claim that the one had demolished the arguments of the other. But I believe now, as a general thing, the several denominations let each other alone, each one pursuing their own line of work. As the Apostles can be endorsed by all orthodox Christians, it ought to be the basis of fellowship for any one of common sense, and a little religion. How these sectarian controversies were viewed by the late Dr. Deems may be inferred from his reply to a certain ecclesiastical bully, who once challenged him to a debate. He simply replied in a note, saying, "I regret any act of my life which led you to believe that I could be made your scavenger." Of all the denominations in N. Carolina, perhaps the Dunkards are the most peculiar. They practice baptism by dipping three times, face foremost, while the candidate kneels in the water, dipping once in the name of each person in the Trinity, so interpreting Matt. 18:19. They keep the seventh day as the Sabbath, practice foot-washing, wear long hair, and kiss each other when they meet for worship. And on their communion occasions, I learn that they have lamb stew, and hand around the soup to the congregation. There is one peculiarity not uncommon with some denominations, as well as individuals, and that is to make a specialty of some point of belief, not more important than other Christian doctrines, but which they make a hobby of, and which they ride, making it the sine qua non of true doctrine, and each one regards everybody else as off of the track, if they don't ride the same hobby he does, some going so far as to unchristianize those who vary from the line of their creed.

The camp meeting has been a great institution in N. Carolina, being held mostly by the Methodists, but of late years these meetings, in most localities, have ceased to be held, and the old encampments are going to decay. Perhaps it is well, for the camp meeting of the present day is not what it used to be. It seems now to be appreciated by many as a resort for social enjoyment, in common with other pleasure resorts, rather than for religious improvement. The great burden on the women at the tent, of preparing the Sunday dinner, and the free entertainment of so many visitors, and the comparatively small spiritual benefits resulting, being considered, it is judged best to dispense with the camp, and hold protracted day services only. The few camp meetings now held in our State, are mostly held in the western counties, except, perhaps, one, which is held annually, on the Island of Hatteras. Many will remember the great camp meetings held in former years, at Rock Spring in Lincoln county, Double Springs in Guilford, Mt. Hermon in Alamance, Union Chapel in Granville, and other places, where thousands have been converted. This writer can never forget Double Springs, as he can say, "This man was born there," and has attended more camp meetings there than anywhere else, and where a number of others were converted who became ministers. This place, true to its name, had two bold springs near by, perhaps not more than four or five feet apart, that supplied the encampment with water. The nick name of that locality was "Cherokee Nation," and it may be supposed that on camp meeting occasions there was some rough material to deal with. There were some "lewd fellows of the baser sort," who would drink whiskey and play cards, around in the woods, during the day, and after night come into the encampment, and play their pranks. Sometimes after the exercises at the stand had closed, and the preachers retired for the night, some of these fellows would slip up to the stand, blow the trumpet, and run off, while others would crow like roosters, around in the grove, one answering the others. On one occasion one of the preachers, in a sermon, likened this class to "bats and owls," that remain in their holes during the day, and after night come out and commit depredations.

In those days there were no trained choirs in the country churches, but the camp meeting singing was grand, as the thousands of voices rang out from the great congregation. And there were some quaint songs that would hardly be appropriate anywhere else. For instance, one was:

"I'll pitch my tent on this camp ground,
O, halle, halle lujah;
And shout old Satan's kingdom down,
O, halle, halle lujah."

and

"Old Satan's mad, and I am glad,
O, halle, helle lujah;
He's lost some souls he thought he had,
O, halle, halle lujah."

and

Great camp meeting over yonder,
On that other shore.
Happy Fathers over yonder,
On that other shore.
By and by we'll go and meet them,
On that other shore."

and

"See Gideon marching out to fight,
And put the Midianites to flight.
He took his pitcher and his lamp,
And smote the Midianitish camp."

While it was a pleasant sight to see those good men and women, with their cups running over, rejoicing in the great congregation, there were some, doubtless, who tilted their cup a little, and let out things that were not very edifying. It is understood that the Methodists believe in "falling from grace," or rather, in the possibility of it, and some perhaps have gotten the idea in their heads so strong as to *practice* the doctrine, and get rather in the habit of falling. So it has been the case that some who professed religion, during a revival, in a year, or perhaps less, have been ready to profess again. One case is reported of a young man who had professed religion several times, and was at the altar as a seeker; and, he soon professed again, when a by-stander said to him, "You came through pretty quick." "Yes," he said, "you see I know how; I'd got it afore." Here may be noted a curious phase of Arminian and Calvinistic faith. The Arminian believes in *knowing* that he has religion, but don't know whether he will keep it, while the faith of the Calvinist does not allow him to know exactly that he has it, but to be certain that he can't lose it.

We cannot judge of the Christian character of any one, merely by observing their movements during a revival of religion. The outward manifestation of feeling, of those under the influence of the Holy Spirit depends much on the constitutional make-up of the individual. Excessive emotional feeling is no mark of high moral attainment. If it were, the colored race would excel the white race in moral character. On the contrary, persons who manifest great emotional feelings are most inclined to instability of character.

As the two extreme sections of N. Carolina vary in soil and productions, so they do in the habits and social traits of the people. Before the war, as there was a larger proportion of slaves in the eastern section, more of the families depended on them for domestic service, and when the war was over many of them still depended on the freed slaves for service, while the women of the western region generally had been accustomed to do their own house work, and often made a hand in the fields. So, when emancipation was effected, they were more independent than those of the east. But the burden on them was very heavy during the war, when so many of the men were absent in the army. I remember, while in the mountains, west of the Blue Ridge, the year the war ended, that I visited a family living in the gorges of the mountains, only reaching the dwelling by a bridle path. The family consisted of the father, an old man, his wife, and four grown daughters, the sons being in the army. All the work of the farm was done by those daughters, even the sowing and reaping of the grain. And then they would carry a sack of wheat to the mill, five miles away, on horseback, over that rugged mountain pass, so steep in some places that I had to dismount, and lead my horse in passing over it; and those girls were the most regular in attending their church, which was five miles distant, sometimes walking there and back home after services. One day, while on a visit to the family, I noticed a rattlesnake's skin stuffed, hanging up by the side of the house, and on inquiry learned the girls had killed it with a hoe, while working in the corn field. One other statement I will make, in regard to my visit there, that I could not have sat down to a table of nicer, more palatable, or better variety of food, anywhere between Richmond and New Orleans, than I found in that log cabin in the mountains.

During the war the coffee drinkers, in the upper region of the State, found a substitute in a tea made of parched wheat, potatoes and persimmon seed, while the people in the low land could fall back on their native herb, the yaupon; and large quantities of sorghum were made, which supplied the place of molasses. While the South, since the war, is designated as the "New South," in view of her advancement in almost everything tending to bring prosperity, North Carolina may be entitled to the appellation of the "New North Carolina," as she has pretty well kept up in the race for advancement.

With the disappearance of the "old flint lock gun," the "tallow candle," and the "goose quill pen," have disappeared other customs and habits that were popular in former years. Mark the advance of public sentiment in regard to the Temperance question. In past years it was not uncommon for prominent church members to run a distillery; and they made whiskey and brandy, and, drank it too. The good old deacon or class leader would set out the bottle to his preacher, when he visited him, who did not scruple to take a drink. But now, where is the church member who would offer it, or the preacher who would take it? And where is the candidate that would risk his election on giving a public treat.

It is known by many that preachers generally have a store of anecdotes, and in their contact with all classes some ludicrous incidents occur. In some communities there are those who attend church, that don't seem to know how to behave, and the preacher feels it necessary to administer reproof, which sometimes requires wisdom and discretion to do properly. Some preachers who are of a nervous temperament, are easily disturbed by such things as crying babies, &c. I will give a case where the preacher, in giving reproof, rather got the worst of it. A well-known Presiding Elder was preaching at a camp meeting, and just in front of the pulpit sat a lady with a little boy in her lap, who began to fret and cry. The preacher, who was known to be rather rough in giving reproof, said to the mother, "Make that child hush." She tried, but failed to quiet him, and the preacher then said to her, "Hold him up there, and I'll make him hush." She did so, and the preacher, leaning over the book board, and looking the little fellow in the face, said, "Hush, sir!" but the boy, looking up at the preacher, said, "I shan't; you hush yourself." A farther contest with the boy was more than he had bargained for, and for once he was non plussed. I was in the company of that preacher a few years ago, and on asking him if that reported incident was true, he said, "Yes, it was a fact."

There are some anecdotes related, at the expense of such preachers as are in bondage to the manuscript, in preaching, &c. It is said by a responsible preacher, that a certain Methodist Bishop, who was very precise in conforming to his manuscript notes, in all kinds of services, was on one occasion invited to offer public prayer at the breaking of ground for a projected railroad, and he had his prayer written out, and an old darkey stood by, with spade in hand, ready to turn up the earth as soon as the prayer was ended. As the Bishop began, the darkey "gazed at him with grinning wonder," and as soon as the amen was said, he grunted out, "Dis is de fus time dis nigger ever hearn of anybody writin to de Lawd on de subjec of railroads." The narrator said the old darkey *broke gravity* as well as ground for the railroad. A certain writer in a sketch of another Bishop, who was known to be a great relater of anecdotes in his preaching, said of him, that he might economize by numbering his anecdotes, that his hearers had become so well acquainted with, and when he wished to use one to say simply, "This is so according to number nine, or ten, as the case might be.

The most remarkable circumstance in connection with preachers relating anecdotes, I ever knew of, came within my knowledge some years ago. It was a N. Carolina Methodist preacher, who was so much in the habit of telling anecdotes, that perhaps it would have been hard to find any one, who had ever heard him preach without relating from one to three or four, or more of them. I think it was the last time I ever heard him preach, that during his sermon he said, "I will relate an anecdote; though I am not in the habit of telling anecdotes." How strange it is, that persons can be so unconscious of their ruling traits. How appropriate are the often quoted lines of Burns:

> "O wad some power the giftie gie us
> To see ourselves as others see us."

It has been said of a certain preacher, that "he selected his text to suit his anecdotes."

It is said there were two preachers who occupied the same territory, a Baptist and a Methodist. The Baptist had gotten up a song, which he sung all around in his travels, which rather gave him the advantage, in popularity, over the other. The song ran thus:

> "Go read the third of Matthew;
> Go read the Chapter through;
> And there it plainly tells you,
> What Christians ought to do."

Then his Methodist rival procured him a song also, to compete with the other, and thus he sang:

> "Go read the third of Matthew;
> Go read the Chapter through;
> And you'll find that John the Baptist
> Was nothing but a Jew."

CHAPTER VIII.

Hospitality—Incidents illustrating character—Some contrasts—Dogs in N. Carolina—The dog at church.

HAVING spent a number of years in visiting from house to house, and having so often to ask for lodging of strangers, I have been in a good position to judge of the character of the people as to hospitality. Let it be understood that by hospitality I do not mean the entertainment of our friends and relatives, or prominent people, by which we might gain notoriety and popularity, nor the entertainment of thieving tramps, or religious impostors; but *that* care and attention to the wayfaring stranger, which is recognized in the scriptures as a Christian virtue. "Be not forgetful to entertain strangers." And "I was a stranger, and ye took me not in," is one of the causes of the sentence to be passed by Christ, of "depart from me ye cursed," upon those who neglect the needy. See Matt. 25:41.

As to general hospitality, perhaps N. Carolina will compare with most of the other sections of our country. But the eastern, or Albemarle region, is unsurpassed in this respect, and Hyde and Lenoir counties may be particularly mentioned, as unexceled by any country I ever traveled in.

But some are to be found in other localities, who furnish examples of anything else but hospitality. In this connection I will note that there are three classes of persons to be met with in traveling, viz; Those who make it a rule never to turn a stranger from their door; those who make it a rule never to entertain a stranger; and those who will entertain people, or turn them away, according to their whims or prejudices, or entertain them for their money. And these characters, which are so much in contrast, and exhibit the good and the bad traits of humanity, are often found in the same vicinity.

On one occasion I called at the house of a man who tured me away just at night, with the statement that he made it a rule never to take in strangers, but that I could stay at a house a mile or so ahead, and on reaching the place found a very kind man, who received me, saying, that he made it a rule never to turn a stranger from his door at night; but he informed me that the man who turned me away from his house was in the habit of sending all callers to him. Now if hospitality is a Christian duty, a man can no more put it off on his neighbor than he can his praying or repenting. I have found by experience that the man who declines to entertain any one, on some frivolous excuse, is generally better prepared for it than his neighbor, who willingly receives him. I can call to mind cases where I have been turned away, at night, from the houses of the wealthy, and entertained kindly by poor men living in log cabins. Upon the whole in these things, it may be truly said, "that where there is a will there is a way."

While journeying in one of the eastern counties, I called at the residence of a doctor, who also was a local preacher, and of course one of the prominent men of his neighborhood, and requested lodging for the night. He began with his frivolous excuses, and said he was a practicing physician, and was liable to be called off at any hour during the night, his language seeming to imply, that if such should be the case, I might take his house on my back, and make off with it. I then made my way to a little village not far off, and called at a little grocery, kept by two brothers, and where whiskey was sold, and though the family was not conveniently situated for entertaining people, I was kindly taken care of, lodging in the store room with one of the brothers. This was a notable circumstance—turned away from the house of the doctor preacher, and entertained by a grocery keeper and liquor dealer!

I will give another case which shows two individuals in strong contrast. While traveling in the western part of the State, I had been invited by the Presiding Elder of the District to attend one of his camp meetings, and the evening before it commenced, and about sundown, I emerged out of the mountain paths into the public road, a few miles from the camp ground, at a quite public place, there being a store and grist mill, all owned by the man living there; and, as he was wealthy, and a prominent church official, I anticipated spending the night with him. But he declined to take me in, saying, they were busy fixing to go to the camp meeting, &c., and directed me to go on farther. I did not take his advice, but drove down to the mill, only a few rods distant, and called on the miller, who lived in a little one-story house, and though a poor man, he said he would do the best he could for me. Having obtained some grain from the mill, and fed my horse at the buggy, I hitched him to the post for the night, at the corner of the house, in full view of the residence of the owner of the premises. After being pleasantly entertained by the miller and his family, I made my way next morning to the camp grounds, where, of course, I felt myself at home. My host, the miller, came also to the camp meeting and met me with a smile, but the man who did'nt receive me into the house was rather shy of me, and I was aware that he felt rather uncomfortable over it, especially as I had him before me on Sunday morning, while I conducted the services of the hour. I had said to my friend, the miller, before coming to the camp meeting, that this man who declined to entertain me would be sorry for it before the end of the week, and said it, knowing what his surroundings would be at the camp meeting. But before the end of the week he left the camp with a sick child, who died in a few days, and I learned that he looked upon it as an affliction sent on him.

Sometimes my patience has been sorely tried, by the complete heartlessness manifested by some on whom I have called to get lodging. On one occasion, my buggy had broken down on the road about sun-down, and leaving it there, I had started to find a lodging-place. It was rainy, and about night, and I had just come out of an attack of intermittent fever, and was getting wet, when I came up to a large farm-house. A young man made his appearance, to whom I represented my case just as it was, when he coolly said he didn't take in anybody. "Then," said I, "can you direct me to the nearest house where any one lives, even a little log cabin, where I can find a shelter?" He said he couldn't tell me. I then said to him, "Do you ever read the Bible?" "Sometimes," he said. "Well, let me read a little of it for you." And I repeated with a vim, "'Depart from me, ye cursed, into everlasting fire, prepared for the devil and his angels, for I was a stranger, and ye took me not in.' Good bye, sir.'" I went on and called at the next house, less than a mile away, and was hospitably entertained by a man who was a new-comer in the neighborhood, and a Northern man.

On another occasion, after being disappointed in finding a lodging-place where I expected it, I came up to a nice looking residence, after daylight down. The man came out and began his excuses, saying, "You ought to have stopped sooner, that they were done supper, and it would be troublesome, &c." I then let out on this style: "This is too bad for a Christian country, that a man has to travel until late in the night without finding a lodging-place. But I'll not insist. Before I would do that, I would kindle a fire out here in forty yards of your house, and sit by it all night. You think I am in a bad predicament. But, though I don't know a foot of the way, and don't know who lives on the road, the Lord has a man ready not far off, who will take care of me to-night." And, sure enough, I had hardly gone a mile until I was kindly welcomed and entertained by a most excellent Christian family. And so I have generally found it, that where I have met with the most selfish and inhospitable man, I have found one in contrast with him not very far off.

The injunction of the Apostle, to "beware of dogs," seems to have been literally obeyed by the law makers of North Carolina, and it seems as if they are unwilling to pass what many would regard as wholesome laws for the benefit of those who think that raising sheep is better than raising dogs. But I do not wish to consider dogs in their relation to sheep, but, as I have found them to be, a disturber of public worship; for, in a number of places the dog has been a church-goer, as well as the rest of the family. And those preachers who are rather nervous, and are disturbed by crying babies, would not be very patient while snarling and snapping dogs were in the congregation. I was at a camp meeting, years ago, where there were a number of dogs on hand, and one night, while the preacher was discoursing on the parable of the Rich man and Lazarus, they were barking and fighting around on the encampment; and, when the preacher spoke of the "dogs coming and licking the sores of Lazarus," he paused and said, "If Lazarus was here tonight, he would have company a plenty."

I will here give an account of a very ludicrous scene which took place at a little meeting house on the mountain. I was visiting the church, which was reached by a little bridle path, as no wheel of any vehicle had ever made a track there. The congregation consisted of about a dozen mountaineers, seated at the back side of the house, and about the pulpit. The little house was built of chestnut logs, and not chinked nor daubed, with puncheon floor and board pulpit, the whole costing, they said, about twenty-five dollars. I had dismounted, and, with saddle-bags in hand, was making my way into the house, when I was met by a little dog, that composed a part of the congregation, which barked vigorously, disputing my entrance. This moved the owner of the dog, an old woman in the congregation, who squalled out at the dog, "git out er here." Then passing on to the pulpit, I paused a little, hesitating whether to take my saddle-bags into it, or leave them outside, as the pulpit was so very small, when an old man at my elbow, the most prominent character present, thinking, I suppose, that I was not used to such an article as a pulpit, pointed to it, saying to me, "You go in there."

CHAPTER IX.

Romance in real life illustrated—Some Temperance stories which illustrate the cause of strong drink—Some cases beyond the reach of Keeley.

MEMORY brings up historical facts, embracing localities and individuals, but as some of the persons are still living, probably it will be best to give only initials. Years ago Miss Lucy B. came from New England to North Carolina, and engaged as a teacher in a college in the town of G., and in the same college there was a German professor of music, Karl P., who was inclined to intemperance. At length he was taken sick, and was confined to his room for some time. Lucy, who was a zealous temperance woman, seemed to take much interest in him, and would send him tracts to read; and although she might have been very disinterested in the matter of his reformation, the gossips said "she was in love with him." Well, he recovered from his sickness and was a convert of hers to the temperance cause. That was before the issue was made for Prohibition, but I think he joined the Sons of Temperance, and, of course, she was still more in sympathy with him. At any rate the matter was still the subject of gossip, and finally caused such a stir up that it resulted in her leaving the college she was in, and taking a position in another college in the same town. Now, while some regard woman as a mysterious and incomprehensible piece of human machinery, and more complicated than the harp of a thousand strings, those who know much of her history will easily arrive at the conclusion of what the outcome would be in the case of Karl and Lucy. Soon it was proven that the gossips were on the right track; and the announcement of their marriage was made, and they left the town, hand in hand, to go into the world to seek their fortune.

They did not leave the State, but located in the city of R., and put up a music store. She continued to be a zealous temperance worker, and was at the head of the Society of the Daughters of Temperance, in North Carolina. During the war, in passing through the city, I remember seeing the sign, "Music Store, K. W. P.," and I imagined how happy she was in her surroundings. But, alas! a dark shadow came over that pleasant home. I have never known how it came about, having lost sight of them for some years. But I was startled at length by seeing, in one of the State papers, the following notice: "Died in this town, in great destitution, K. W. P., of Raleigh." Then followed the statement that he had left his home, intending to make his way back to

Germany, but reaching the town of G., he was taken sick and died, and was buried by the Masons. No mention was made of his family, or what had become of his wife. But the circumstances indicated, what has happened over and over again, that he had turned to drink, then cruel treatment of the wife, &c., and finally, that he had left her intending never to return. So time passed away, and I had no information of Lucy, until a few years afterward, when I noticed her name among the graduates of a Medical College of the North. Of her career since, I know nothing. How eventful has been her life! We may here moralize a little. Some of her experience was the result of a blunder made by other women besides her, that of marrying a reformed drunkard. And many girls have acted more foolishly than that, in marrying a drunkard and expecting to reform him after marriage. And though many of them have on this account drank of the cup of sorrow, yet doubtless others, with such examples before them, will do the same thing.

Recently the ground has been taken that drunkenness is a disease, and if so, then it must be hereditary, as is also claimed. As an illustration on this point, a lecturer not long ago gave us the following incident; A man was taken with delirium tremens, and a physician was sent for, but when he arrived the man was dead; and one of his relatives, his wife or sister, went out to meet the physician, and said to him, "O! doctor, you have come too late." And he replied, "Yes, madam, two hundred years too late." His answer implied that the case of his great-grandfather ought to have been attended to. If this idea is correct, what a motive is here presented for total abstinence, especially to every father, in the fact that the dram drinker is entailing upon his offspring the constitutional tendency to drunkenness! The Keeley Institute is based upon the assumed fact that drunkenness is a disease, and the Keeley cure is now offered as a remedy. But neither Keeley nor any other man, can prepare a drug that will work the moral reformation of a drunkard, and his remedy will fail in the case of every man who does not *will* to quit drinking. Those who take the remedy, and are not cured, are such as do not want to leave off strong drink; and such as have lost will power, are beyond the reach of Keeley.

I can give a case that illustrates this point. I knew a young man, years ago, handsome, prepossessing, and of much promise, who became a physician, and entered into practice, but after awhile took to drink, and before long became a confirmed drunkard. After the lapse of some years, having sunk lower and lower in intemperance, he was induced to go for treatment to the Keeley Institute. On his return home he professed to be cured of the appetite for strong drink; but it was not long before he took to drink again, and to other debaucheries, proving that the only remedy for him was, for the One that made him to make him over again, or completely regenerate him. Before long he got into a drunken debauch and invaded the home of a respectable family, and behaved so outrageously that he was indicted, tried and convicted, and sentenced to labor in the chain-gang, among other convicts. And such a spectacle he presented, while working on the public roads in shackles, was a good temperance lecture to young men, if they will receive it. This victim of strong drink recently served out his sentence, and the next thing heard of him was, that as the "dog that was turned to his own vomit again, and the sow that was washed to her wallowing in the mire," so was he.

On one occasion, while in the Albemarle region, I came to the humble dwelling of a lonely old widow, who was quite poor, and, being quite communicative, she gave me a kind of history of her life as the wife of a drunkard. As may be supposed, she was strongly opposed to intemperance. Although she was illiterate, she had rather a talent for writing verses, and showed me a poem she had composed, on the miseries of the drunkard's family. It was a very pathetic production, though in doggerel rhyme. I can only remember one stanza, the last one of her poem, the idea of which she had taken from the following incident: A habitual drunkard, who had made many promises of reformation, and had failed to keep his promise to drink no more, on returning home one day called for an auger. It was brought to him, and to the astonishment of his family, he took it and commenced boring a hole in the side of the house; and when he had finished it he stepped back, and pointing to it, said, "when that auger hole grows up, then I'll take another drink." And the old lady concluded her poem in the following language:

> "I'll bore a hole in my house so high,
> That all may see it, as they pass by;
> And when that auger hole grows up,
> Then I'll buy wine and take a sup."

CHAPTER X.

Marriages in North Carolina—Laws and customs concerning it defective—Primitive marriages more rational—The clergy officiating on such occasions a relic of Romanism.

IS it not a remarkable fact, that, while marriage is the oldest institution in the world, in the nineteenth century of Christian civilization, in our country, the laws and customs concerning it are so loose and defective? Perhaps there is no other country on the globe but these United States, where there is no uniformity in the laws regulating marriage and divorce. Take, for example, Illinois and South Carolina. If a man wants to get rid of his wife, he has only to go to Chicago, and sojourn there a little while in order to get a divorce, while in South Carolina, he can get none for any cause, not even that which Christ recognized as sufficient. But in North Carolina a man can get a divorce for causes not allowable by Christ. And the Methodist Episcopal Conference here has forbidden its ministers to officiate in the marriage of any who have been divorced for any other cause than that which the scriptures sanction as justifiable. Before I ever saw North Carolina, I had heard that it was the place where people went when they ran away to get married, as Justices of the Peace are not allowed to marry people in Virginia. And so North Carolina has afforded better facilities for clandestine marriages than some other places.

The idea given us of marriage, by Christ, is, that it means the union, for life, of one man and one woman, instead of one *boy* and one *girl*, but according to usage here, a man's fifteen year-old daughter may be kidnapped and carried off, contrary to his will, and the marriage effected hastily at the house of a magistrate, or in some public road, and that is generally the end of it. It is true, that it is contrary to law here to issue a marriage license, or marry a couple, where the girl is under age, without the written consent of the parent, but this is remedied by the simple process of a falsehood in regard to the girl's age, by the friend of the kidnapper who applies for the license; and, although the parent has the right to prosecute the offending parties, and annul the marriage, yet he submits as the choice between two evils, the daughter having already gone off to live with the man, or boy, as the case may be.

Here let us philosophize a little on the subject. The celebration of marriage by a minister or magistrate is where the evil comes in. Compare the present marriage customs with those of past years. When Christ attended the marriage of

Cana, he was there simply as an invited guest, and no Rabbi or Priest had any part in it. From the parable of the Ten Virgins, it will be seen that marriages were celebrated *in the home* of the bride, and there was no such thing known as a clandestine or runaway marriage. And where, and how, and why, has such a change been brought about in regard to this matter? The answer is very simple and plain—It is due to the corruptions of the Romish church. This great ecclesiastical hierarchy by a decree made matrimony a sacrament of the church; and from that time in every country where Roman Catholics had control, marriages were legal only when celebrated by a priest at the altar of the church. So the whole ceremony of marriage was transferred from the home to the Romish church, and monopolized by the priests, and made a source of much revenue. Then it is very clear that the idea of a minister of the church being necessary in the consummation of marriages originated in the falsehood of matrimony being one of the sacraments of the church.

In the great Reformation from Romanism, why did not the Protestants include a reformation in the matter of Romish marriages? But this so-called "sacrament" was perpetuated in the Church of England, and has been made the fashion in the Protestant Episcopal church. The most sensible way of celebrating marriages, outside of the home, was practiced by the Quakers, who required the parties to be married to come before the church at their monthly meeting, having given previous notice, and there acknowledge each other as husband and wife, and that finished the ceremony.

And now, in this country, the State comes in and monopolizes the business, requiring a license to be taken out, authorizing some officiary of the Church or State to consummate the marriage. In the case of an elopement, what a farce is enacted in the reading of the ceremony—"If any one can show just cause, why these two persons may not be lawfully joined together, let him now speak, &c." when at the same time, the parents or friends of the girl who has stolen away from home, if present, would object and prevent the marriage, are probably in their beds asleep. There was lately some movement made in view of memorializing Congress to pass a uniform law regulating marriage and divorce throughout the United States, which if done would be wise. And if such a law should embody the requirement that previous notice should be given of all intended marriages, it would cut short all runaway marriages. The business of celebrating marriages is not monopolized by the clergy here, as it is in

Virginia, any township magistrate being authorized to celebrate it; yet it is rather the fashion or style, especially in high life, to have the favorite preacher to be master of ceremonies, while sometimes it takes two to finish it off. One thing in the interest of the officiating minister is the marriage fee, which in some cases, where there is wealth, is a considerable item. But in many cases the preacher comes off minus his fee. Some preachers can relate rather amusing incidents in their experience in this line. One had married a young fellow, who asked the preacher what he charged, and when told that he was not in the habit of making a charge, said, "I'm much obliged to you; I'll do as much for you sometime." Another, after the ceremony was over, told the preacher he wanted to pay him something, "but he didn't have any money; he hadn't sold his rabbit skins yet, but when he sold them he would pay him."

Some of the preachers have suggested a plan to head off such close-fisted fellows as try to dodge the marriage fee by asking the officiating minister what he charges. The suggestion is, that when such a one asks that question, to reply, "Well, we leave that to the bridegroom. If he thinks he has gotten a valuable wife, that he estimates pretty highly, he can give a right good fee; but if he thinks he has rather a kind of twenty-five cent wife, then he can pay accordingly. This would put such a fellow in rather an awkward predicament.

CHAPTER XI.

Marriage itself—Some comments and suggestions—Some illustrations.

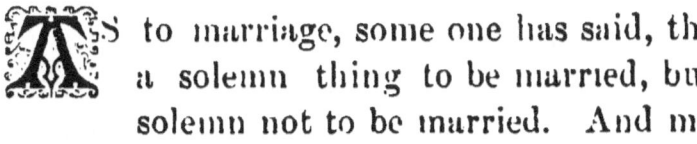S to marriage, some one has said, that it is a solemn thing to be married, but more solemn not to be married. And marriage has been likened to a lottery, or chance game, as to whether one gets a good husband, or wife. According to Holy writ, he that gets a good wife "obtaineth favor of the Lord;" and, if so, when a man gets a bad one, where does *she* come from? The woman was given to the man for a help-meet, not a help-mate, as many improperly quote it, but a help that is meet, or fit, as the word signifies; and when this idea is carried out, then marriage is the earthly paradise; and, if otherwise, it is purgatory, if we know what that is. Marriage has been often perverted from its proper intent, to unholy purposes, resulting in discord, and often divorce.

In slavery times young men, on being introduced to young ladies would ask, "How many niggers has she got?" and there were some bachelors in those days known as regular "fortune hunters." Of course, that game is played out now, in North Carolina, but some American heiresses, who travel in Europe, furnish pretty good game for the old broken down aristocrats, who condescend to marry them for a few hundred thousand dollars, while they are pleased to barter themselves and their money for a title; and it is a matter of record that some of them have reaped the fruit of their folly in the miseries inflicted by a brutal husband. There is also a good deal of romance about marriage. We have cases of "love at first sight," followed by hasty marriages, and more than one case has occurred in North Carolina, within my knowledge, where respectable girls have answered advertisements for a wife by men living a thousand miles away, and afterward they have met and were married. In such cases it is hard to tell which exhibited the greater folly, the man or the woman. But, stranger still, I have more than one case in mind, and one of recent occurrence in a neighboring town, where the married persons separated and were divorced, and afterward were remarried.

Surely, when it is considered how far-reaching

are the consequences of marriage, it should be entered into with carefulness and judgment, as well as fancy, and feeling should be exercised in it. And not only should character be considered, but it should be borne in mind that there is such a thing as the law of heredity, by which constitutional tendency to disease, intemperance, and other vices may be transmitted from the parent to the child. In this connection how appropriate is the application of the proverb, "an ounce of preventive is worth a pound of cure." But, after all, where is the man or woman, who is wise enough to secure himself or herself from an unwise choice in contracting a marriage? Is it not a remarkable fact that the wisest man who ever lived, and one who had married more wives than any other man on record, should have made the most complete failure of any other man? Of course, I refer to King Solomon, who had seven hundred first-class wives, and three hundred second-grade, making a thousand in his household, and fourd not one true woman among them all. This indicated in Ecc. 7 chapter and 2 verse. And these strange wives led to his backsliding from God. See 2 Kings 11:1, &c.

The present discussion of the "woman question" may result in seriously affecting the marriage relation. The divine law has assigned to the woman her position, and the latest inspired deliverance on the subject is that of the Apostle; and if in 1 Tim. 2 chapter, and in Eph. 5 chapter he does not mean to teach that the woman must be in subjection to the man, then there is no sense in the English language. But with the progress of events the woman seems to be moving to the front, or rather up toward the head. Already we have female pastors of churches, and the last political campaign witnessed the novel sight of a woman from a thousand miles away, making speeches, as the colleague of one of the presidential candidates. As to how far woman may go in religious work, of course she cannot come up to the standard of scriptural qualification for ordination, as she cannot be "the husband of one wife." But perhaps in regard to her public exercises, it may be safe for us to occupy the position taken by a prominent teacher, when a noted woman preacher was holding a special meeting in his town. On being asked what he thought about a woman's preaching, he said, "Well, as to whether Mrs. M. is called to preach or not, I am not able to decide; but there is one thing I am entirely satisfied of, and that is, that I am not called to stop her."

Here I will say that the great moral issue of prohibition in North Carolina, is likely to be affected by another phase of the woman question. I refer to the question of woman suffrage. The idea has never been popular in the South, and while the temperance people of North Carolina have been very generally united on the question of prohibition, heretofore, yet now the prohibition party has included woman suffrage in their platform. And so prohibition having tacked on to it other measures, upon which Christian men are divided, and many do not endorse, the natural result is a division in the prohibition army, and many life-long prohibitionists will not co-operate with that political party. It will not do the cause of prohibition any good for extremists, who are in the minority, to sit in judgment on other Christians of unblemished character, who differ from them, and unchristianize them, because they do not vote with their political party.

One fact in this connection I will note. A recent General Conference of a Methodist body, has made women eligible as delegates to their ecclesiastical bodies; and in their revised book of discipline, have left out the word *obey*, in the marriage ceremony, as applicable to the bride. But that avails nothing, for leaving out the word obey, the woman promises to live with the man "after the ordinance of God," which requires her to be in subjection to her husband.

As to the marriage of young people, the best that can be done is to train them up with right views and principles, but as to giving them advice after they have set their heads on marrying, it is a vain thing. They will hardly ever take advice on that subject, even after asking it. In my younger days I had no better sense than to offer advice to young lady friends, cautioning them to beware of a certain class of young fellows, thinking I was doing them a favor, instead of committing the unpardonable sin in their sight. So my experience has cured me of that kind of work. It seems that in courtship there is a kind of mutual deception practiced. Each one has on their Sunday clothes, and their Sunday manners, and the business is carried on with smiles, and compliments, and each one liable to be mistaken in the real character of the other.

While it is true that people are so averse to taking advice in regard to marriage, perhaps there is no subject that young people need advice about more than they do in this. But more especially is this true in regard to young girls, as disappointment in love affairs, results in more damage to them, in many cases wrecking their hopes of happiness for life. They should remember how many of their sex have come to grief, by listening to the fair speech and promises of plausible men.

Every girl of good sense should be prudent enough not to put her character in the keeping of any living man. They should bear in mind that many young men are inclined to boast of their influence over girls any way, and even in cases where one is partial to a particular young man, if she crosses the line of prudence, she should not be silly enough to think that her reputation will not be established, among the rest of the young men of her acquaintance, as she showed herself to be in the sight of that young man. I will take the liberty to say, that in the present state of society, parents allow their daughters too much latitude in their association with young men. The fact is, it is too much the fashion nowadays to let girls figure as women before they are really out of childhood; and some of them, while they should be in short dresses, are pretty well tutored in the practice of the "Arm clutch."

Years ago there was a family of several daughters, and one grown son, who was the eldest, and who was looked upon by his sisters as a model young man whom they looked up to, as their counsellor. On one occasion, in trying to impress upon them how guarded they should be in the company of young men, he said; "Remember, my sisters, that every man in the world is a grand rascal, and your brother among the rest." This was of course, an extravagant remark, but was calculated to be impressive. Yet the impression did not much exceed that of King David when he said, "I said *in my haste*, all men are liars;" while some writer has said that, "if David had said it at his leisure, he would not have missed it much."

Here I will make some suggestions to that class of young people who are honest and sincere in regard to marrying. To the young man I will say, if you have really fallen in love, or in other words, become infatuated, don't imagine that you have found an angel. Remember that there are no angels down in this lower world, and though we believe there will be women angels among the redeemed in heaven, you should not believe that the one you are about ready to worship is one, unless you can see her wings, and not then, for it might be an imitation article. You had better not flatter you idol into the belief that she is a superior being, or she may fancy herself too good to marry an ordinary mortal like you. You had better simply let her know that you regard her as a nice, amiable woman, who will make you a good wife, and that she is the woman of your choice. And if she should say, "no," don't threaten to hang or drown yourself, on your way home; and don't go whining around about it, but show as much independence as you can, and if she repents afterwards, you will be very apt to find it out. In this kind of business, sometimes final perseverance works wonders. Women as a rule in marrying seem to disregard equality, either financially, socially, intellectually or morally, and are governed more by their fancy for the individual man, and marriages are continually taking place where there is the greatest contrast in these things.

Perhaps the most of persons have observed that the law of contrast prevails, as to those who marry, in size, complexion, temperament, &c. To the young marriageable girls I will say, is is the best not to be in much of a hurry to get married, or you may have to repent at leisure. If marriage is best for you, the right man will come along after awhile. Only continue in the path of duty and wait for him. Don't say you don't aim ever to marry, for no man, who knows much of human nature, would stand back on that account. And you need not manifest any anxiety about it, for an amiable, good looking woman will carry with her the power of attraction. On one occasion a young lady acquaintance of mine asked me if I could tell her the "best way to set her cap." "O yes," said I, "I can tell you exactly. Just appear as if you were not setting it." This fact may be confirmed by a single Scripture quotation; "In vain is the net spread in the sight of any bird." And the interpretation is, if we wish to catch a bird, we must not let that bird see us spreading the net.

As women do not have a fair opportunity, always, of knowing the character of the man they marry, they are the more liable to be deceived. I will here give a little historical sketch. I had a relative, who had married two clever men, and was left a widow the second time with a considerable estate, and being a fine looking woman of about forty, it may be supposed that she would be attractive to impostors. Before long she was visited by a widower who was recommended to her by some person in his town. He was polite and genteel in his manners, and on preaching days would ride with her in her carriage over to the village church, she being one of the prominent members. She married him, and so completely had he gained her confidence, she did not reserve any part of her estate to herself. Then he showed himself as he was, not only a drunkard, but an Universalist in his belief, and was vicious, and abusive toward his wife; and not only did he refuse to go to church himself, but would not let her go, and would ridicule her favorite preachers. He was wasting her estate very fast when his career ended, and he died with delirium tremens. After his death I visited the widow, who gave me an account of her experience with him, and what abuse she received from him, even having her life threatened, and being driven from her home during the night. If she ever manifested any inclination to marry again I never knew of it.

CHAPTER XII.

The public roads in North Carolina—How some people give directions to travelers—Quaint names of some localities—Some personal adventures, and curious characters met with.

THOSE who have traveled much in North Carolina, by private conveyance, will testify to the fact, of the little attention paid to the condition of the public roads. It is no uncommon thing for wagons to be mired down, up to the axles, and have to be prized out with fence-rails. I remember that a few years ago, after crossing a creek with horse and buggy, the horse sank in mire up to his hips, and could not be gotten out until I went to a house, and obtained a hoe and spade, and *dug him out*. The plan of keeping up the public roads here, has been by having an overseer, as he is called, who notifies the hands, at certain times, and they gather in and work the roads in a kind of fashion according to law, and often the newly worked will be a sign that court is coming on the next week, which puts one so much in mind of some people who neglect the work of repentance until about the time they have to die, and go to judgment. And the matter of putting up sign-boards is much neglected, also. How worrying it is to a traveler, on searching the forks of a public road, to find no sign to indicate which road he should take, when it would take so little trouble to nail up a small board with a few words on it, giving the necessary information.

And how strange it is that so many seem incapable of giving sensible directions to a travler. How annoying it is for one to inquire the way to a certain place, near night, of a strapping young fellow, and to be told ; "You go along down across the creek, and go on till you get passed granddaddy's, and then you'll take the left hand," &c. And often people will say, "Just take that road, and keep on straight, and you can't miss the way," and perhaps one will not go far, before they will find a plain fork, and one road just as straight as the other. I remember, on one occasion, calling at a house to get directions, and an old lady coming to the door, I had to pass through the following ordeal. On asking the way to the house of Mr. B., she said, "I spose you're a stranger about here." "Yes madam, and you will please give me directions about the road." "Well, yes; and is he a kinsman of your'rn." "No, madam, no kin at all; but you will please tell me the way to his house." "O, yes; and what might a body call your name?" Well, after so long a time I managed to get her kind of directions.

In passing about over North Carolina I have come across some curious names of localities, and some odd characters, and have had some personal adventures, not marvelous encounters with bears, wild cats, or rattle-snakes, but such as are outside of our common experiences of life. While traveling in the Albemarle region I found myself in "Paradise," then in "Pellmell," and in "Snakebite;" the later place not so named because some one was bitten by a snake at that place, but because a reckless fellow, in one of his frolics, there engaged, for a wager, to "bite off a snake's head." And in the mountains there is Beau Catcher's Knob, so named, perhaps, because some girl, once upon a time, caught a beau there. And there is Sandy Mush Creek, so named, the people said, from the fact that in the early settlement of the country, some hunters camped on that creek, and, in making mush from the water of the creek, they got some sand in it; so afterward it received the name of Sandy Mush Creek. Then we have "Shoe Heel," and "Lick Skillet," and "Love Lady," the origin of which I have no account of.

There is one case in which tradition, so called, proves to be a myth. In passing from the Albemarle Sound, some years ago, in a schooner, to Roanoke Island, the old captain, among other yarns, told me what, he said, was the origin of the name, "Croatan." He said, away back in years past, the people stampeded from the place; and there was one woman left behind, whose name was Ann; and that she starved to death, and was eaten by carrion crows; and as crow ate Ann, the place afterward was called Croatan. But this pretty little story is spoiled by the historical fact, that when the colony containing the parents of Virginia Dare, and left on Roanoke Island, was lost, the only tidings ever heard of them was the name "Croatan," carved on a tree on the Island. So it is certain that the place was named Croatan from the earliest knowledge of it, by the English.

I had an adventure, over on the border of Virginia, with one of the most unique characters I ever met with. It was late in the evening, and I was getting nearly out of the settlement of the well to do people, and was aware that for miles there was but little chance of finding a lodging place for the night; and according to directions, I called at a comfortable looking residence, and being informed that the old man was down at the barn, feeding, I awaited his return. Then I spoke to him, telling him I called to get lodging for the night, and the following dialogue took place between us. In a crabbed way he asked, "Why didn't you stop back yonder?" "Well," said I, "I was directed to call here." "O, yes, I reckon you were." Then I said, "just direct me to some place where I can find lodging for the night. He said, "there isn't any place." Then he asked, "what's your name?" On telling him my name, he asked, "what's your occupation?" Here I hesitated, telling him he would find out more about me around the fireside. This, I suppose, rather aroused his suspicions, and he said, "Yes! a gambler I expect; and drunk at that." "Well," said I, "I should like to know how you can tell when a man is drunk that you never saw when he was sober." He said, "O, I can tell; I've been a drunkard myself." Then he said, "Unhitch and come in." I told him I didn't feel inclined to do so, unless he was in a better humor. But at length I decided to take him at his word, and find out more about him. So I unhitched my horse, he leading him to the stable, and I following; and as he led the horse toward a stall he pointed to a cutting room, where a small darkey was cutting feed, and said, "You go in there and go to cutting feed," and added, "may be it will sober you some." I kept in a pretty good humor, knowing how he would be taken down when he came to know the facts in the case. So I went into the cutting room, and took a hand with the little darkey in cutting the feed, using the old style cutting blades, which was rather a tiresome job, and I stopped awhile, when the old man approached, and tried to hurry me. Then I spoke very plainly, and told him if he didn't mind I would hitch up, and leave him, and report him to others. But, said I, "suppose you find that you are mistaken in your ideas in regard to me." "Well," said he, "if I am, I'll ask pardon; but I don't think I am."

By this time we were called to the house, and by the time he reached the table, he was in a humor good enough to "say grace." And, mind you, it was a Methodist family. On being seated at the table the old lady, by way of apology, said she had been living with the old man forty years, and had hardly got acquainted with him yet. There was also a grown son and daughter at the table, and on hearing my name, they remembered me, having attended a special meeting held by me not many miles distant. By this time the old man, though very deaf, began to get some light on the subject, and taking his seat in the corner, began a kind of soliloquy. "Well," he said to himself, "I said if I was mistaken I would ask pardon." I found the family kind and hospitable, and the next morning, on fixing up to start, the old man said, "you mustn't think much hard of me; if you had told me who you were, I wouldn't have talked to you so." One fact my experience with the old man impressed me with, namely, that he did not practice any deceit in his intercourse with people.

A curious character was old Mr. L. in the lowlands. He was a real Paul Pry, and in trying to satisfy his curiosity, would pump any body, any where, and on any occasion. Perhaps he never had his curiosity satisfied in a more ludicrous manner, than he did on one occasion, in the vicinity of his own home. He went to the postoffice, and as he walked into the room, the proprietor was just in the act of drinking a glass of Seidletz powders. The old man, true to his ruling passion, plied the question; "What kind of a drink is that you are taking?" And being told what it was, he asked, "And is it a pretty good kind of drink?" And being informed that it was, he said, "would you let me have a taste of it?" "O, yes," the man said, "I'll fix you up a drink."

So the postmaster concluded to satisfy his curiosity in playing a trick on him. So he brought two glasses, and putting one of the ingredients into one of them, he handed it to him, saying, "drink this." And as soon as he had swallowed it, handed him the other tumbler, with the other portion of ingredients, saying, "Now drink this;" and he did so. Of course the mixing and the effervescence took place in his stomach, and the reader may imagine what capers the old fellow cut, as, with distorted countenance, he jumped up, stamping, and snorting, while the effervescing fluid poured out of his mouth and nostrils! And it is hardly necessary to say that his curiosity was fully satisfied as to what kind of drink that was.

Those who travel much by private conveyance, and among strangers, need not expect always to find one at night to take them in, and sometimes much inconvenience is experienced. But my experience has been, that whenever I have been turned away by a crabbed "Nabob" at stopping time, I have hardly ever failed to find a clever family not far off, whose hospitality was exhibited, in contrast with the want of it in the other. And my experience in traveling has gone far to establish in my own mind the truth of a special Providence. On one occasion, while traveling in

Nash county I had, as usual, a box of Bibles, with an oil cloth cover, and had also an extra box in my buggy, without any covering to protect it from the weather. In a little while I saw a heavy cloud arising out of the west, but felt not much concern about it, thinking it was going around me, but in a little while was surprised to find a heavy rain in sight, and swiftly approaching me, and as no dwelling was near me, I saw no way of saving the books from being ruined. I halted, and behold, an object I never saw before or since, within less than five steps from me, namely, a little board or box house, in a corner of the fence, about four or five feet square, placed there evidently as a shelter in case of a storm, for the protection of those who worked in the field near by. It was only the thought of a moment to alight and take my box and valise into the little shanty where I kept dry, while almost a cyclone raged without; and the rain was soon over, and I came out and went on my journey. Again the next week I passed the place, and was thinking of the strange occurrence, and before going far the rain began to fall, from a cloud overhead, and unexpectedly, while no family was living near. But just at this time I found myself in the road opposite an old unoccupied house, with open door, and hastily hitching my horse to the fence, I went in; and the worst hail-storm I ever knew raged for more than an hour. If any one should say all this happened by chance, then the conclusion is that chance provides for us in cases of great emergencies.

Once I was returning to the neighborhood of Plymouth, from the Island of Hatteras, by way of Hyde county. It was in the month of May, and landing in Hyde, from a schooner, I was afoot, with some seventy miles, or more before me in reaching my destination, by the public road. But after going some miles, I received information that there was an old canal, which had been cut from Beaufort county through the Big Swamps to the Plymouth road, and if I could get some one to put me through in a canoe, it would save me more than half the distance to Plymouth. So when I reached the vicinity of the canal I succeeded in engaging two darkies to put me through, which they would have to do by pushing the canoe through the canal, a distance of ten or twelve miles. We procured an old cast off, leaky canoe, and I took my seat in the fore-end, with a gourd to dip out the water when necessary. To appreciate the journey, it will be well to give a little description of that canal, so called, which was simply an old ditch, with about two and a half feet of water, with obstructions here and there, in the way of sunken logs, &c., while it was bordered on both sides with an almost impenetrable thicket of cane, brambles, &c. We started about 2 o'clock, P. M., and our speed may be imagined, when it is known that, while the two darkies propelled the canoe with poles, I did the double duty of pumping out the water, and guiding it by pushing it off from the projecting logs and stumps, and sometimes having to rid myself of the bamboo briars that hung overhead, and became entangled around my neck. To make a long story short, about sun-down we reached near the end of the ditch, when the canoe was grounded on an old moss covered log, and I landed there, leaving the darkies to make their way back as best they could, while I had to make two or three miles through the marshy swamp, in order to reach the Plymouth road. And after reaching it I sat down to rest, only to engage in a battle with the mosquitoes. But it was some five miles to Plymouth, and night being upon me, I preferred to find a place under the pines, and laid down and slept pretty well; not like Jacob, with a stone for my pillow, for there are none in that country, but made a substitute of my valise. Early next morning I set out, and reached the house of a friend in Plymouth in time for breakfast; and, washing off the mud of the swamp, I reached the church in time for the Sunday morning services of the Methodist District Conference. But this was not the only time that I had to spend a night under the long leaf pines, on the borders of a swamp. I remember being in just such another predicament, only it was not in the balmy month of May, but in the winter season; but I made me a roaring fire of pine logs and knots, and after eating my supper of crackers, I laid down, with my over-coat and valise for my bedding, while the voice of the great owl, and the "Chuckwills Widow," broke the stillness of the scene. But, says one, "were you not afraid?" Here I will suggest an antidote, to fear under such circumstances. It is the words of David in the Psalm. "The Angel of the Lord encampeth round about them that fear him and delivereth them."

CHAPTER XIII.

Some other curious characters and things noted—Life, and how they live, in the two extreme sections of North Carolina, contrasted.

AMONG the curiosities of the past years, which are passing away, is the old style pulpit. How strange to think what kind of places were constructed for the preacher to address his audience from. It was a very proper expression, to speak of going *up* into the pulpit, for the preacher did have to go up, and pretty high up too, to get into it, reaching it by a stair-case: and, having a door to it, he could shut himself in. It seemed like the people wanted the preacher to be as far removed from this lower world as possible in discoursing to them of heavenly things; and perhaps no one thought of the disadvantage of speaking from such a place. Daniel Webster is represented as having said that, one evidence to his mind of the divine authority of Christianity was, "that it had succeeded in the world in spite of pulpits." It has been stated, that while a preacher was discoursing from one of the old pulpits, who was full of action, and spinning from one side to the other, a little boy sitting by his mother, thinking that the preacher was fastened up in the great high box, whispered to his mother, "Ma, why don't they let him out?"

And the old cemeteries, what quaint epitaphs they contained! It will not be in good taste to criticize the spelling; but having copied a number of them, I will give a few here, which I think are good. Perhaps most of persons have seen a very common one, which represents the dead as saying;

"Remember, man, as you pass by,
As you are now, so once was I, &c.

One reads;

"O cruel death, thou hast conquered me,
And by thy dart I'm slain;
But Christ my Lord has conquered thee:
In Him I'll rise again."

On the tomb of an infant.

"We bring them, Lord, with grateful hearts,
And yield them up to thee.
Rejoiced that we ourselves are thine—
Thine let our offspring be."

On the tomb of a mother.

"Sweet is the sleep our mother takes,
Till in Christ Jesus she awakes.
Then will her happy soul rejoice,
To hear her blessed Savior's voice."

Perhaps the rarest thing in the way of church building I found on the banks of John's River, which was two houses of worship side by side, only a few yards apart. The fact itself suggested schism and church division in the community; and I learned that the first house was built by the Baptists; then the Second Adventists came, and proselyted some of the members, and it resulted in the building of another church for the Adventists. This is evidence that religious liberty is *a fact* in our country. We are glad that, while we have corruption in politics, we are free from that curse of the old world, the union of Church and State; and that religion cannot be monopolized by civil or ecclesiastical tyrants, by whom many have suffered martyrdom in the past. Even under the influence of the so-called Reformed Church of England, just before the Revolutionary war, in this country, Quakers and Baptists were prosecuted and whipped as disturbers of the peace, because they offered to preach the gospel in plain dress, and without the gown and book, and without the sanction of the state church.

But while religious liberty is guaranteed to us, under our constitution, yet there are people among us, bigots, and if they had the power, would not allow others to advocate any faith different from their own. Perhaps some may be surprised to know that there are churches in North Carolina, claiming to be primitive in faith, who will not permit their members to participate in a Sabbath School, and cases can be located, where they have excluded persons from the church for doing so. And I can name another case, where they arraigned a member on the charge of making public prayer in a meeting of another denomination, and on his failure to make acknowledgement for doing so, they expelled him. It will not be a surprise to any, perhaps, to know that the denomination referred to is described in ecclesiastical history as "becoming extinct." In this connection I will mention that, while canvassing in the eastern counties I called at a house, and on telling the woman my business, she said; "Are you one of these fellows, goin' about the country baptizing babies? If you are, I don't believe in no sich." Of course, one might conclude that the Pedo Baptists had not had much of a showing in that latitude.

Now, in order to show the contrast in opinion, I will give an incident which took place up in the mountain region, and which placed me rather in a ludicrous position. It was on Saturday evening that I made a visit to the family of a relative, who were Episcopalians. They had a church building not far off, but no resident minister; but I found a visiting minister there, who was to preach at the church the next day, and the mothers of the babies that had been accumulating there for some time were to be on hand, and make use of the opportunity to have them baptized, and among the rest was a married daughter in the family I was visiting. Of course, I expected to attend church with the family, though I had never witnessed the Episcopal ceremony in baptizing infants. Well, on Sunday morning, things were astir, all hands getting ready to go to church, when I was approached by the married daughter saying, "Cousin D., I wish to ask a favor of you, but I don't know whether you will be willing to do it." Thinking perhaps she wished the use of my horse, vehicle, or something of the kind, I replied, "Certainly, cousin, anything I can do for you let me know." Then she said, "I want you to stand god-father to my baby to-day." A clap of thunder out of a clear sky would hardly have surprised me much more. The god-father business was a new role for me to appear in; so I told her, perhaps I might not attach as much importance to it as she did, and besides, it appeared to me as rather a droll piece of business for a Methodist to stand god-father to an Episcopalian baby, that he had never seen before, and might never see again. So I persuaded her to get a substitute, and when in the ceremony, I found what the god-father was required to promise for the child, I was glad I was out of it.

I must not omit to notice one of the most singular and mysterious personages who ever appeared in North Carolina. This was an old Frenchman who took up his residence in Rowan county, and engaged in teaching school. He was known as Peter Ney; and he was represented as a man of fine education and of noble bearing, but quite eccentric. He was not communicative in regard to himself. It was rumored that he was some distinguished man in his native country, and perhaps had to leave for some offence. He had no family, and I think he died in Rowan county. Then the story was circulated that he was the celebrated Marshal Ney, of Napoleon's army. But the strangest thing about it was, that according to history, Marshal Ney was court-martialed and shot, in France. But the mystery is cleared up, if the following statement is true: "That in carrying out the sentence of the court-martial, through the influence of the Masons, the muskets were loaded with blank cartridges, and when the soldiers fired on Ney, he fell, according to the arrangement, and his body (not his corpse) was taken charge of by his friends, and he was conveyed away, and afterward came to America, and found his way to North Carolina. The truth of this statement is strengthened, from the fact that, quite recently, the subject has been brought before the people in a lecture on Marshal Ney, in which the lecturer undertook to show that the old French school-master was the veritable Marshal Ney; and if this be true, this "truth is stranger than fiction."

It has been said that "one half of the world don't know how the other half lives." And the saying is doubtless true, in its application to the two different sections of our state, where there is so much difference in their habits of life, &c., and where the people in one extreme section know very little about how they do live in the other section. It has been my lot, during past years, to be entertained in the mansions of the rich, and again to be seated at the table of the poor, with the house-pig under the table.

It seems as if the law of compensation generally prevails, and where one section is deprived of advantages possessed by another, they enjoy some other good things the other is deprived of. For example, in the eastern section of the state, they have mosquitoes, chills, and fever, and inferior water to drink. But they have an abundance of fish, oysters, and the most beautiful and level roads to travel over. And in the mountain region, while they are deprived of the good fish, oysters, &c., they have an abundance of the best water, milk and butter, honey, fruit, &c. Take as an example also Hatteras and Roanoke Islands. The soil there being mostly banks of sand, does not yield a support for the inhabitants, but their granary is in the water, and they have simply to get in their sail-boats, and go out into the waters of the sound, get a load of fish, oysters, &c., and run over to the nearest town or village, across the sound, and dispose of their cargo, and get their supply of provisions and groceries.

To compensate for the barrenness of those

islands, the country bordering them produces corn, rice, potatoes, &c., in abundance. But though Hatteras does not yield any food supply, it produces some articles of trade. There is an abundance of the Yaupon-trees growing there, and they gather quantities of the twigs and leaves, and kiln-dry them, and put them up for market, the tea of which is considerably used by the people in the lowlands. I remember years ago in the Albemarle region, I was present at a church, on Saturday of a special meeting, when at the close of the services a deacon arose and made the following announcement: "I will say for the information of the friends and brethren, that there is a vessel down at the creek loaded with oysters, yaupon and mullets."

Another peculiar growth on Hatteras island is the palmetto, the same of which the palm-leaf fans are made. It grows in vast quantities there; a single stem springing out of the ground will expand, and flatten into great leaves, or fans, from three to five or six feet in length. It is a wonder some one has not gotten the idea of putting up a fan factory. There is yet another article of trade there. While trudging along through the sand one day, I met a boy with an ox-cart, loaded with bones, and on inquiry, found that they were porpoise bones, that had been lying on the ocean beach since the last fishing season. But where could a market be found for bones on that island? Well, I found that they were then engaged, and were on the way to be delivered to the captain of a schooner, anchored in the sound, which was there to gather up the bones for one of the fertilizing companies.

We may judge that the men of wealth and leisure, who come to the North Carolina coast to shoot game, do not practice the methods employed by the natives. I learned while there, that their plan was to provide themselves with what they called "hip breeches," which was simply a pair of rubber boots, with legs reaching to the hips; and having provided also one or more domesticated fowls, to be used as decoys, they would wade out into the shallow water of the sound, and, fastening the decoys to a stake, retire a few rods to a blind, made of bushes, and waiting until a gang of wild fowls were attracted to the place by the decoys, they would get a good shot at the whole gang. Sometimes, when they cannot have fowls for a decoy, they substitute artificial ones. I came across two very good imitation ducks, where I spent the night near the Pamlico Sound, made of wood, and which had been used as decoys. One bird peculiar to these waters is the sea-gull. People down there informed me that these little fowls feed on clams. But it would seem rather a puzzle how they manage to get at a clam, which is incased in a shell, fully as hard and thick as that of an oyster; but I was told that the gull first takes the clam in the beak, and flies with it high up in the air, and lets it drop upon the hard sandy beach, and repeats the operation if necessary until the shell is broken, and then devours the clam.

And I found on the Hatteras beach also the funniest little creature I ever saw, which they called a "Sand Fiddler." It had a shell body, about the size and shape of a crab, with prominent little shiny black eyes, and very long legs, and a plenty of them, which were out of all proportion to the body. They were quick of motion, and seemed able to run backward as well as forward. They lived in little holes dug in the sand, and would run into them on the appearance of any one, and if intercepted would turn and make for the water, when a rolling wave of the ocean would hide them from view. I don't know why they are called "fiddlers," for they seem better adapted to dancing than fiddling.

The land lies so low in that sea-coast region, that while there is a plenty of water, there is no water-power; so they cannot have water-mills; but they construct wind-mills, which are built in the open fields where there are no trees to obstruct the wind. The mill-houses are of one story, and are built on one large post for a foundation, and made to turn on a pivot, so that the house, with its long arms and canvas wings, can be turned to suit the variation of the wind. As water obtained from wells there would be too salty to drink, cistern or rain-water, generally obtained out of a trough placed under the eaves of the house, is used, a conch shell answering the purpose of a dipper. But they seem to be as contented and happy as they are anywhere else, and they certianly are as religious as the people in any other part of the state.

I visited Roanoke Island at the time of their Superior court, Manteo, the county seat of Dare, being on the Island, and I never before attended such a quiet and orderly court. The court was convened about 2 o'clock, P. M., on Monday, and adjourned the next day at about 5, P M. I inquired how it came about that such short sessions of court were held there, and the reply was, "No liquor is allowed to be sold on the island." So much for Prohibition in Dare county. I will note an incident here. On a visit I made to the representative, who introduced the bill for local option in the legislature, he informed me that after some controversy the opposition agreed to admit the bill, provided that an exception be made in the case of the public house at Nag's Head, allowing them to furnish liquor to their guests during a stated period. So in this way the bill was passed. I will here note a tragedy. Captain M., who lived on the island, was a useful man, and well disposed when sober, and he made a visit to Nag's Head about Christmas, in an open boat, by himself, and did not return home. The only intelligence that could be obtained in regard to him was, that after indulging in drink, he left Nag's Head late in the afternoon, for home, the winds being high. Of course the particulars could not be known, only he was a victim of Nag's Head whiskey.

In contrast with the smooth running of the streams in the low-lands, the moving of the water being hardly perceptible, is the rushing and roaring of the streams over the rocks in the mountain region. In crossing the Blue Ridge once, I noticed a little grist-mill that had no dam or race, and was turned simply by the little stream running down from the mountain, and pouring its volume of water upon the wheel.

The beauty and grandeur of the mountain scenery of western North Carolina seems not to be appreciated or realized by the natives of that region, perhaps from the fact that they have been familiarized with it all of their lives, while it strikes a stranger with all the force of its natural beauty. I do not remember ever beholding a more beautiful spot than the valley of Pigeon River, in Haywood county, where the stream, as clear as crystal, runs through the flat land farms, while the great mountains are piled up all around at a very short distance.

CHAPTER XIV.

Lost in a mountin gorge, in a pitch dark rainy night—A preacher in an awkward predicament—More personal experiences—An extraordinary "Fish Story," &c

I WAS returning to my head-quarters, which was four or five miles from the summit of South Mountain, and being on the opposite side of the mountain, had to cross it in order to reach there, which was by a little bridle path. I had reached the summit about sunset, and already a black cloud indicated an approaching rain-storm; but on I went, and soon the rain was pouring in torrents, while the night closed in upon me, and after getting about a mile down the mountain, I got out of the path, and dismounting and walking and stumbling over rocks, and brush, and trying in vain to get into the path, the prospect seemed fair for me to spend the night in that dark valley. I remounted and sat in the saddle while the rain continued to pour in torrents, and Egyptian darkness prevailed around me. But finally I decided to retrace my steps to the top of the mountain, where there was a settler, depending on my horse to keep the path, I reached the summit safely. I rode up to a log cabin, and was received out of the rain, my horse being stabled in a rail-pen. But the prospect was a poor one for lodging, for the house was occupied by two families, and there were only two beds, and I could not expect to have a bed to sleep in; so I leaned my seat back against the ladder, that was used as a stair-way to "the loft," and putting one arm between the rounds, and locking my hands together I fixed myself the best I could for a nap. But after awhile the man of the house approached me, and insisted on my lying down, saying they had fixed a place for me; and I laid down, not knowing exactly how many bed-fellows they expected me to have; but the man occupied the bed with me, while his wife sat up by the fire all night. This was unsurpassed hospitality. Of course they were very poor people, and I left by daylight next morning, and went down the mountain, reaching my destination in time for breakfast.

If a man travels much, his experience, no doubt, will have a tendency to increase his faith in a special Providence, and that God's care is extended over "the stranger." An incident occurred in my experience, which, if not a providence, was a happy co-incidence. It was immediately after the surrender, and I was passing over the Sandy Mush mountain on horse-back. I had picked up a canteen stopper in the road, by which I knew that returning soldiers had passed over the mountain. My thoughts turned to the fact that I had lost my pocket-knife, and I felt the need of one very much. Then the thought came into mind, "Why couldn't I find a knife?" And the desire arose in my mind so strong that I determined to begin looking for one; so, turning side-ways in my saddle, and leaning over, I fixed my eyes on the foot-path by the side of the road, and so rode on slowly down the mountain; but I think I had not gone a quarter of a mile before my eyes fell on a good size pocket-knife, lying in the path, and I alighted, without any surprise, and put the knife in my pocket. How strange that my thoughts should be turned to the subject of a pocket-knife, just before reaching the place where one was lying in the path!

In another part of the state an incident occurred within my knowledge, in which a preacher was placed in the most awkward predicament, perhaps in view of delivering a discourse, of any case on record. He had held a special meeting in the vicinity of a North Carolina town, and on closing it, on Sunday afternoon, made an appointment to preach at night in a church in the town, and supper time found him at the table of the pastor of the church. After supper, having made a hasty call, he started for the church, and while some distance off, the second bell was ringing. To save time he made a bee line for the church, through back streets and by-ways, when he came to a bluff, and down into a flat; and making a step on what he took to be a smooth sandy plain, he found himself on his all-fours, in a slough of mire and muddy water, and getting out with feet and ankles, hands and wrists covered with mire, hurried on, and in that plight found himself at the entrance to the church, in which was the waiting congregation. It would be hard to find a more awkward dilemma for a preacher to be in for discoursing to a congregation, especially when as yet he had no text selected. But it was the work of a few moments to hasten across the street to a well, where was a bucket of water, and scooping it up with his hands, to wash off the worst of the mud. Then walking into the church where the pastor was waiting for him, he requested him to conduct the preliminary exercises, during which time he found a text; and the discourse was delivered, the congregation being none the wiser for what had happened. Perhaps to make this an honest narrative, it is proper to say that the actor in that scene was this writer.

I will give an incident, showing what a contrast there is in character, even between members of the same family. I called at a house, the home of an old lady and her grown daughter, and both came out to meet me, and on inquiry I found that the daughter had a bible, but she said she would like to get a hymn book, and thinking I might advise her in regard to getting one, I inquired what kind she wanted. She said "Primitive Baptist" was the kind she wanted. "O!" said I, "I didn't know there were any of that denomination about here." "O yes," she said, "there are a good many of them about here, and they have a church about a mile off." Then I said to the old lady, "That is a very small denomination, and they are put down in history as becoming extinct;" and added that I had known one of their preachers, who was a man of some education, and of influence, in the adjoining counties, and that had it not been for him, there would not have been so many of them in that section of country.' This rather nettled her, and turning upon her heel, she left me, saying "You'd better said if it hadn't been for Goddle Mighty." Then the daughter spoke in a soft, mild manner, saying that she was partial to that denomination, and that her father was a Primitive preacher. So I found I had been talking to the widow of a Hard Shell preacher, and concluded that I had better beat a retreat; but I was much impressed with the contrast in disposition between the mother and daughter.

On another occasion I came across another family, where I think I made a better impression, and doubtless did some good. I called at the house about night, and requested lodging, the family consisting of a widow and a grown son and daughter. The young man at first made some excuse, but the sister interposed in my behalf, and I was taken in. On going to the supper table the daughter, on learning that I was engaged in the work of the Bible Society, said she used to read the bible, and was a member of the church, but she had gotten into trouble, and had quit reading it. I told her the bible should not be neglected, but should be sought for consolation, &c. The conversation was continued afterward, around the fireside, and I told her that our trials would result in good to us, if we would bear them in a proper manner; and I referred her to the 12th chapter of Hebrews, trying to make a proper application of it. After awhile I heard her say to her mother, "Ma, I wouldn't have had this man to miss stopping here for five dollars." Next morning, before I left, having become more free and unreserved, she gave me the particulars in regard to her trouble. She had been engaged to be married to a young man, the time had arrived for the marriage, and the supper was prepared, when he failed to appear, proving false to his engagement. And when I learned that the young man was inclined to dissipation, and that there was a streak of insanity in his family, I told the young lady that I was sure she would live to see the day when she would thank the Lord that she had escaped from being tied to such a man.

I have hardly ever met with an outspoken atheist or infidel, in my travels, though in a few instances I have found one pretending to be such. While so many claiming to believe in the Christian religion are immoral in their lives, it would be absurd to expect one who rejects it to possess anything like a decent morality. On one occasion I came up to a store kept by a young man, who on learning my business, came out to me saying, "I want a Bible," adding a profane expression. "Yes" said I, No doubt you need one very badly, and I would recommend you to study the ten

Commandments the first thing, especially the one forbidding to take the name of God in vain." He said, "who is God?" "Well sir," said I, "He is represented in the Bible to be the great self-existing and eternal I AM, infinite in wisdom, power, and goodness. That is about all we can know of Him; and now, if you assume to understand all about Him you will be about equal to Him and be a god yourself." I then told him I knew what was the matter with him, that he had been reading some infidel stuff that had been refuted again and again. He admitted that he had been reading Voltaire. On leaving him he expressed a wish to have more talk with me hereafter, and wherever I met him he was very respectful toward me. I will add that an acquaintance of his told me, that when he was at College he had made a profession of religion, and had charge of a class in the Sabbath School.

About the hardest criticism of our country's noted infidel, is by H. L. Hastings author and publisher of Boston. One of the Christian Advocates quotes him thus: "I have heard of a man traveling around the country exploding the Bible, and showing up the mistakes of Moses, at two hundred dollars a night. It is easy to abuse Moses, at two hundred dollars a night, especially as Moses is dead, and cannot talk back. After hearing the 'mistakes of Moses,' it would be interesting to hear a military leader and legislator like 'Moses the man of God,' who after he was eighty years old commanded for forty years an army of six hundred thousand men, emancipating, organizing, and giving laws to a nation, which has maintained its existence for more than thirty stormy centuries, give his candid opinion concerning the 'mistakes' of a 'Colonel' of cavalry whose military career is said to have included one single engagement, in which 'he was chased into a hog yard, and surrendered to a boy of sixteen;' after which, as soon as exchanged, he heroically resigned his commission in the face of the enemy, subsequently turning his attention to managing swindling whiskey rings, discussing theology, defending scoundrels, blaspheming God, and criticizing dead men who cannot answer him."

Perhaps the most extraordinary occurrence in my experience, is what I will call a "fish story," and happened in my youthful days. I was very fond of fishing with hook and line, and late one evening I took a line with a single hook on it, and baiting it, put it in a mill-race near by, tying the line to a bush on the margin, thinking I might find a fish on it the next morning. On going there in the morning and taking up the hook, I found two fish on it, a cat-fish and an eel. They were tangled and twisted into a bundle or knot, the eel being coiled around the cat-fish. After considerable trouble in untwisting the tangled knot, I found that the hook was in the eel's mouth, while the cat-fish was strung on the line, through his gills! I looked at the spectacle with astonishment, and was perplexed to know how such a thing could have happened. Finally I decided that there could be but one way to solve the mystery, viz that the baited hook was discovered by both fish at the same time, that the cat-fish got it first, and in his eagerness to swallow it, it slipped through his gills, and that the eel seized it immediately, and swallowed it. If it did not happen in this way, how did it happen? And did any one ever know of two fish being caught on a single hook at the same time?

Here I will mention a very curious fact in animal life, namely, a dog that crows like a rooster. He is a small dog, and his owner lives only a few miles from my home, and brought him here the other day, while on a visit. I learn that it was not natural with the dog to crow, but he acquired it by imitation; and so, after awhile, succeeding so well in his mimicry, when the rooster crowed he would crow also. Let us give three cheers for the little dog Dash.

Most of our readers perhaps have read of Jasper, the negro preacher in Richmond, and what amusement he has afforded the people by his persistence in setting forth his belief "that the earth does not turn over, but that the sun moves around the earth." But every one is not aware that there are a number of grown-up white people in North Carolina who believe the same thing; and they are the good pious ones too, who believe so, and they appeal to the Bible for proof of it, their chosen scripture being the account of Joshua commanding the sun to stand still. They seem to lose sight of the fact that the miracle of stopping the rotation of the earth would answer the purpose of Joshua without his understanding Astronomy.

One is represented as saying, that if the earth does move "the Lord would have told us so in the Bible." It would be equally as good reasoning to say that if the Lord had wanted us to know Arithmetic he would have put the multiplication table in the Bible. The old adage may come in here: "If ignorance is bliss, tis folly to be wise."

In my travels a few years ago, I spent the night with a man who was the greatest curiosity in the way of a bald-headed man I ever saw. He had not a single hair on his head or face, not even any eye-brows or eye-lashes. On inquiry I learned that he, and a brother, when they grew up, had each a good head of hair, but both took a curious kind of disease, and all their hair came out, and never grew out any more.

And another rare curiosity, to me, I found about the same time in passing down from the mountain country. I was spending the night with a family of young people, the man being about twenty five years old, and his wife, I judge, not much over twenty. She said they had been married five years, and on asking her how many children she had, she said, "eight in all," which rather surprised me, but going to give particulars, after naming her first born, she said, "One time there were twins, and another time THERE WERE FOUR." That struck me rather with wonder, for I never, in all my travels, had come across such a family as that. But she assured me that she had FOUR living boy children born at *one time.* It is such an uncommon case it will not be out of place to say that the lady in question was the wife of Mr Payne, who lived near the Island-Ford on the Catawba river.

CHAPTER XV.

Some experiences in the mountains about the close of the war—Evading a controversy—Incidents of the Prohibition campaign of 1881.

SINCE my last visit to the mountain region, and the line of Railroad has been extended there, much advancement has been made in almost every line. Asheville, as I remember it, was only a little village, about like the average County seat. During the war there was not as much quiet among the citizens as in other parts of the state, for sometimes the territory would be occupied by Federal troops, and the Confederates would be refugees, and again the Confederates would come in, and the Union men would leave and go inside of the Federal lines; and so the people lived in a state of unrest, though as neighbors, they lived in as much friendship with each other as anywhere in the state, where they differed in sentiment, in regard to the war; and I will ever bear in mind their charity in this respect.

Of course general education had been neglected, and many were illiterate. I visited a man who was a licensed preacher down toward the Tennessee line, and seeing that he had a few books on a little shelf, I asked him what kind of books he had. He said he had the Bible and Hymn book, and the "Tracts Amtresock." The name striking me as a novelty in the book line, I asked him to let me see it, and he handed me down a volume of bound Tracts, published by the American Tract Society, and as there was not room on the back for the whole title, it was abbreviated thus, "Tracts. Am. Tr. Soc.," which he called "Amtresock," and his wife said, "Its a mighty fine book, the Amtresock is; we like it mightly."

The region around Asheville used to be famous for runaway marriages, and as the territory was occupied by the South Carolina and the Holston Conferences, quite a number of the Methodist preachers married in that county. An old minister, who had married and settled in Buncombe, told me *that* circuit was known among them as the marrying circuit.

It is a fact that the people of the upper part of the state are naturally more excitable than they are in the lowlands. This is observed in religious revivals, the people in the western part of the state manifesting much more emotional feeling. I have been struck mith some of the rare expressions, of a figurative character, I have heard from some of the old brothers in the mountains, during their religious exercises. In a prayer meeting I heard one pray that the Lord would give them a "Benjamin's mess" and another that he would "give them a kid to make merry with their friends."

The use of the expressions, "we uns" and "you uns" has been referred to by others, and I have noticed another phrase used by persons in their salutations of each other. In response to the inquiry, "how are you?" instead of saying, "I am well," they will say, "I'm stout." I once heard the following salutation and response. A neighbor approaching a house, to a woman at the door; "Good mornin; how's you uns." The reply was, "We uns are stout, are you uns stout?"

There used to be one peculiar article of trade in the mountains, which was ginseng root, that grew wild in the woods. It was dug by the country people, and sold to the merchants, who shipped it, its destination being China, where it was in great demand. The people called it "Sang," and I have seen women and children coming to the store with little sacks of it, asking, "Do you want any sang?" And the merchant would give them the price they paid for green and for dry sang.

In the valley of Pigeon River there was a man, who was a Universalist; and he was very active in circulating his "no-future-punishment," and "no-hell" literature in the community; and learning of his movements, on my visit to the church in that vicinity, I published that on my next monthly visit I would discourse on the "everlasting punishment of the wicked in the world to come." In the mean time I learned that the Universalist referred to was a considerable controversialist, was very over-bearing, and had obtruded himself on a former preacher at that church. Well, when I reached the church on the appointed day, I found that he was present, and his disciples, and quite a large congregation, though I had never formed any acquaintance with him. Before going into the church, a young man took me aside, and informed me that it was reported in the vicinity that the Universalist was to be there that day and reply to me. I stated to the congregation, before commencing the services, that I expected simply to do what I promised to do, namely, to deliver a discourse on future punishment, after which the services would be closed. The discourse was delivered, the congregation dismissed, and with saddlebags in hand, I was making my way out of the church, when on reaching the door the Universalist approached me smilingly, saying, "As no one will introduce me to you, I will introduce myself;" and as soon as he could begin with any show of decency, while the surrounding crowd waited to see what the outcome would be, he said, "Only one side has been heard to-day." In reply I said, "I can decide the matter in two minutes. I have just discoursed on the subject, and said all that I have to say at present, and you can preach on it too when you get ready." He said he "couldn't get a congregation to hear him." "Well," said I, "I can't help that," and thus leaving him, I went off with a brother to dinner. I will say that the plan adopted to rid myself of the adversary was approved of by the people.

During the campaign for Prohibition in our state in 1881, my home was in the middle section of the state, and in a community where there was much of the Anti-prohibition element, embracing "lewd fellows of the baser sort," who were violent in their abuse of the friends of temperance; and prohibition, and anti-prohibition meetings were held in the country around. I will note some incidents that may have an influence on the side of truth. An anti-prohibition meeting was held nearly at my door, the orator of the day being a lawyer of dissipated habits, who not long afterward died a victim of strong drink. While the subject is a grave one, (and who can doubt it, when so many are being brought to the grave by intemperence,) I will give rather a humorous incident. At the time an anti-prohibition rally was held in the town of Oxford, I met an old darkey on the street, and he delivered himself on this wise: "No, sar, I aint a gwine to hab my rights taken away from me; I been read in my Bible bout Esau dat sold his birth-right for a mess of *partridges*; and when I told him it was pottage, and not partridges, he said, "Well, I bin read it so in my Bible." Some of these anti's were so illiterate they called prohibition "probation."

A prohibition meeting was held in the northern part of the county, participated in by two well known lawyers of Oxford, and several ministers, a noted distiller, he of course, an anti-prohibitionist also, being present. Well, after all of the speakers had made addresses giving their reasons for prohibition, one of the lawyers, Mr. V., arose, and said, if there was any anti-prohibitionist present, who objected to what had been said, he had the privilege of speaking; and Mr. T., the distiller arose, and spoke zealously against prohibition, but unfortunately referred to the Scriptures, saying there was no such thing as prohibition in the Bible, and when he had finished his speech, Mr. V. arose to reply; and then came the skinning. The speaker called attention to the fact that the first law ever enacted for the government of mankind was a prohibition law, namely, that given to Adam in Eden, "Thou shalt not eat of that tree." &c; and that the first anti-prohibitionist in the world was the devil, who came along and told Eve, "You won't die sure enough. The Lord knows that this fruit will just make you wise, and be as gods, and then you'll be about equal to him. He just wants to take away your privileges. So the devil was the first one in the world to set himself against God's prohibition law." Then the speaker, referring to Mr. T., said, "he has more prohibitions laid on him than any man in this county. I don't say that Mr. T. will steal, but the government presumes that he will, and employs a man to watch him, and measure every drop of liquor he makes, and he doesn't have the control of his own distillery, the government agent is holding the key; and all these prohibitions are laid upon Mr. T."

Rev. Mr. H., one of the speakers, gave an incident, showing the ruinous effects of strong drink. He said he had married an amiable young woman, to a young man of fine promise, and they began house-keeping with good prospects of a happy life; but after awhile he began to drink a little, and the habit grew on him until he became a confirmed drunkard. The speaker then said that on one occasion he was passing the home of that once happy couple, and as he came near to the house, he heard a noise, and the door opened, and he saw that man kick his wife out of the house, and down the steps; and she approached him and begged him to protect her from the man that strong drink had changed from a husband to a demon!

CHAPTER XVI.

The status of Christianity in N. C.—How far, as a people, are we Christianized?—The optimistic and the pessimistic of things.

WHATEVER may be said of the state of Society in North Carolina, is true, more or less, of any other section of our country. Within the borders of our state are more than twenty of what are known as orthodox denominations, whose ministers preach the gospel to the people in every section of the state, and embrace perhaps over half a million of church members with thousands of organized Sabbath Schools, Missionary and other benevolent societies, with missionaries laboring in foreign lands, while every year thousands of converts are reported as the result of the labors of the different pastors, and evangelists. This view of things would indicate the complete evangelization of the people of the whole state at an early day.

But there are some adverse facts to be considered. First, is the development of Christian character in the churches, equal to the ratio of the converts reported? Who can say that it is? It cannot be expected that new converts will begin a Christian life on a higher plane than they find in the church when they come into it. Query, how far is the membership of the churches advanced in the *practice* of what Christ taught as the standard of Christian duty? How far is the golden rule observed? And which predominates in the life of the average professor of Christianity, the self denial enjoined, or self indulgence?

Of course, the religion of the present day is fashionable, and popular, and walks in "silver slippers," or rather in many cases in "*gold* slippers," and no one is persecuted on account of religion, or for the want of it. Toleration prevails, and a little too much of it, perhaps, for there are evils tolerated that ought not to be. It is a telling fact that corporations, controlled by so called Christian men, grossly and wilfully violate the holy Sabbath. The Sunday railroad trains, as they go thundering along, proclaim their disregard of the laws of God. And the rottenness of what is called "Society," with its punctilious observance of the rules of etiquette, is continually showing itself by the scandals which indicate the immoralities practiced in social life, even among those who have had a standing as members of popular churches. And an example of this kind is now being exhibited to the world by a scandalous civil suit at the Capital of the Nation. And the record of crime to-day is unsurpassed in the history of the country.

Why is there such a demoralization of society in this land of Bibles and of churches? As an evidence of how far below the standard of Apostolic Christianity we are, mark the deliverance of the Apostle, in 1 Cor. 5:11. Here Christians are forbidden to fellowship such characters as far as to keep company with or to eat with them. And are not these sins so popular that they are not recognized, and in many cases retained in the church? Is it not a standing reproach, that in this country, which has reached the highest intelligence, such scandalous sins prevail as the heathens were rebuked for by the New Testament writers?

Although the gospel has been so fully preached throughout the country, there must be a good deal of ignorance and self delusion prevailing among those professing Christianity. Is it possible that a man can be an idolater and not know it? And yet the Apostle declares that "Covetousness is idolatry." And this sin leads to extortion, as well as to other sins, and is classed by the Apostle with drunkenness and theft; yet I never heard of any one being arraigned before any church on such a charge, though the apostle declares that such shall not inherit the Kingdom of God." See 1 Cor. 6, 10.

Where is the dividing line between the world and the church? If it is not where the worldly drink, and dance, and indulge in the vain extravagances of fashionable life, where is it? And if in all these things professing Christians conform, where is their identity as "a peculiar people?" Is the world in the church, or the church in the world? I will call attention here to a discrepancy between what is New Testament morals, and that which is recognized in our country by society generally, namely, that a woman is required to possess a higher standard of moral character than a man, in order to be received into society. The word of God declares that, "His ways are equal," and that "He is no respecter of persons." Then he makes no distinction between a male and a female sinner; and both are accepted of God on the same conditions. The same sin that will exclude a woman from heaven, will exclude a man, and in the final judgment

Christ will make no distinction between a he goat and a she goat. Then what right has any set of people to make a different rule in regard to male and female character? Women have it much in their power to remedy this thing. When they require of men the same standard of moral character, in order to receive them as associates, as men require of them, then may they have more influence over them for good, and start a reformation along this line.

I will relate an incident which affords a good example of moral courage in a young lady. It is related "that there was a young man of wealth, but of dissipated habits, who imagined that any girl would be glad to have his company, and on a public occasion he approached the lady in question, and offered her his arm. While she was a strong temperance advocate, she was a girl in humble circumstances; but she simply drew back from the young man, saying, 'I thank you, sir, I make it a rule never to poke my arm through a jug handle.'"

It will doubtless be accepted as a truth, that where the religion of Christ is established more fully, there woman is most respected and honored, and where demoralization prevails she is the principal sufferer. Since I have been in North Carolina, there has been a record of many crimes, that have passed out of memory, but there are others which have occurred, which can never be effaced from the memory. It seems really a crime great enough, for a man to blast the character of a young girl, destroying her hopes of happiness for this life, and then forsake her; but it is a crime of diabolical and peculiar atrocity, when the criminal, in order to get her out of his way, decoys her from her home, under the pretense of marrying her, and in cold blood murders the defenseless one.

There is a tragedy of this kind in the annals of North Carolina, which occurred in past years, and which is commemorated in the name of Naomi Falls, on Deep River, in Randolph county, which is so named in memory of Naomi Wise, who was drowned in the River there by Jonathan Lewis; and Naomi was buried in sight of the Falls, and only a few hundred yards distant from the village and Cotton mills of the "Naomi Falls Manufacturing Co." The memory of Naomi Wise has also been kept alive in the minds of the people in the country, by the Song of "Poor Naomi." From published accounts, I will give a short sketch.

Naomi Wise was an orphan girl of some nineteen years of age, and has been described as a beautiful girl of medium size, handsome figure, expressive countenance, and winning manners. She lived as a domestic in the family of a country farmer. Among her visitors and admirers was Jonathan Lewis, who belonged to a daring and reckless family. He gained the affections of Naomi, and she fully confided in him. But in the mean time he had a flattering prospect of a marriage with a young lady of superior future and station; and the rumor having been started of his relation with Naomi which was calculated to damage his prospects with the young lady in question, he made up his mind to get rid of Naomi. Then the powers of hell posessed his soul, and he became "a devil incarnate." So he called on Naomi, pretending to wish to marry her without delay, and agreed to take her to a magistrate for that purpose. They met at the spring that evening, according to agreement, and she mounted on the horse behind him. But instead of making his way to the house of the magistrate, he carried her to the Falls of Deep River, and riding into the stream, he threw her from the horse into the rushing waters, where no doubt he thought she would sleep and disturb him no more. But the sentence had gone forth, "Be sure your sin will find you out," and the cries of Naomi were heard near by, and messengers were sent to the river, and her lifeless body was drawn out of the water.

The guilt of Lewis was fully established, and he was imprisoned in the jail at Asheboro, to await his trial. But he soon escaped from his prison and fled to the west, and remained there a number of years, but they got on his track, and had him rearrested and brought back to North Carolina for trial. He was acquited, as there were not living witnesses to convict him, and he returned to his home in the west. But his "damnation slumbered not," and he died soon afterward. Perhaps it may be a wholesome thing to give some account of his last hours. "After all hope of his recovery was given up, he still lingered. He seemed to suffer beyond human conception. The contortions of his face were too horrid to behold. His groans were appalling to the ear. For two days the death rattle had been in his throat, and yet he retained his reason and his speech. Finally, he bade every person leave the room but his father, and to him he confessed all the circumstances detailed. He declared that while in prison Naomi was ever before him. His sleep was broken by her cries for mercy, and in the dim twilight her shadowy form seemed present with him, holding up her imploring hands. Thus ended the career of Jonathan Lewis. No sooner was his confession ended, than his soul seemed to hasten away; yet not away from the hell that burned within him, but doubtless to that hell which has been prepared for the devil and his angels."

The song of "poor Naomi" contains eight stanzas, and though not possessing any literary merit two stanzas of it will be given here as a specimen.

"Come, all you good people, I'd have you draw near;
A sorrowful story you quickly shall hear;
A story I'll tell you of Naomi Wise,
How she was deluded by Lewis's lies.

Naomi was missing they all did well know,
And hunting for her to the river did go;
And there found her floating on the waters so deep,
Which caused all the people to sigh and to weep."

A superstition prevailed among the people of the vicinity, that in the dusk of evening a song may be heard about the river, in accents low and sweet, beginning;

"Beneath these crystal waters,
A maiden once did lie. &c.

In more recent years the vicinity of Deep River witnessed a similar crime, and poor Martha Pinnix was the victim. She too confided in one who decoyed her from her home, and instead of going to her marriage, she was shot through the head. And though the best talent of the bar could not evade the evidence of the murderer's guilt or shield him from conviction, and the death sentence, yet he escaped from prison and fled to a foreign country.

Again, another such case occurred of more recent date, and Peggy Isely was the victim. She likewise thought she was going to her marriage, and left home with her deceiver, and afterward parts of her remains were found in a burnt log-heap in the low-grounds of her murderer. He was tried and convicted, and I was present when he expiated his crime on the gallows. Some noted circumstances happened in connection with that execution. One incident verifies the fact that crime often proves its own detective. After the murdered woman had been missing for some weeks, a few persons were gathered at a house in the neighborhood, and the murderer not yet suspected, being present, some one remarked how strange it was that nothing could be heard of the missing woman, when he said; "You just as well try to make out like I had killed her and burnt" —and, bethinking himself, cut short the sentence. But it was enough, and getting the idea of the woman being burnt, search was made, resulting in evidence of her being murderered, and burnt in the log-heap. While there was not the least doubt of the guilt of the convicted man, he declared under the gallows that he had nothing to do with the murder "in any manner, shape or form." And a Hardshell preacher held religious services over him, and laying his hand on his head, said, from what he had told him of his experience more than twenty years before, "I have no doubt but he is a child of grace." What a ridiculous doctrine to proclaim to a crowd, perhaps of a thousand people, that the cold-blooded murder of a defenseless woman cannot hinder a man from being "a child of grace." In this case the criminal had been raised under the same kind of a creed, and had been heard to say that he believed that every man had an unalterable destiny, and if any one felt inclined to do anything he might just as well do it, for it would not alter his destiny at all.

The brutal murder of Miss Turlington, and the mysterious disappearance of the accused, also a deaf mute, is fresh in the minds of the people; and a still later victim was Ellen Smith, whose murderer was executed recently, at Winston. These murderers of helpless women were not of the illiterate class, and most of them were of rather prominent families. Surely, no greater criminals were ever born in North Carolina.

CHAPTER XVII.

Hindrances to the advancement of Christianity in our own country—The follies and vices of society at the present day.

CONSIDERING that the gospel is preached so fully from so many pulpits, and so many means of grace are afforded to every class of people, the general demoralization of society must be the result of counteracting and demoralizing influences outside of the pulpit and the Sabbath School. What are these influences? First of all must be noticed, defective family government and training of the young. In many families there is no religious instruction afforded, and the want of family government is so plainly visible, that the scripture injunction, "Children, obey your parents," would have to be transposed into "Parents, obey your children," to suit the practice in many families, where the parents obey their children more than the children obey them. The fact is, the children of this generation are allowed to assume the habits of men and women entirely too early, and boys, especially, are brought under bad influences, outside of home, which the parents are innocent of, and if they are not careful to know where they go, and what company they are in, perhaps it will not be long before they will inquire sorrowfully, "Where is my wandering boy to-night?"

Another bad influence exercised upon our youth is the vicious literature. Parents should watch, and see what kind of circulars and papers their children get from the post-office. See the notices in the so called literary papers, published in New England and elsewhere, offering to send "sealed circulars," &c. An idea may be formed of how much of this poisonous literature is circulated from the reports of Anthony Comstock, the agent of the "Society for the prevention of Vice." The intoxicated boy of fourteen or fifteen years, or the cigarette smoker of ten years, indicates what the future harvest will be unless there is a reformation along this line.

In considering the follies and vices of our day, let us begin with those habits where there is the least appearance of evil. There has been recently established in eastern North Carolina, a "chewing gum factory," turpentine being the chief ingredient used in the manufacture of the article. This indicates the prevailing habit of gum chewing, which prevails mostly among the young, though not altogether confined to them. I remember on one occasion in Eastern North Carolina I called at a house, and the old lady came out to meet me, while she was vigorously chewing gum, and after awhile a grown daughter came into the room, and she was chewing it also, and then the old man came from the field, and as he approached, behold, he was chewing it too. This gum-chewing seems like an innocent habit, and the gum a healthy article, but the excessive exercise of the glands of the throat will exhaust the saliva, and after awhile the result may be indigestion and dyspepsia. But there is a ludicrous side of the business; "Say, Mister," said a little child, to a man who had charge of a number of cattle that were chewing the cud, "do you have to buy gum for all them cattle to chew?" Evidently the child recognized the similarity between cattle chewing the cud, and people chewing gum.

Foremost, and greatest of all demoralizing influences, and which is so fatal in its effects, is that of strong drink. In the old "blue back spelling book," Noah Webster said, "Alcohol destroys more lives than war, pestilence and famines;" and doubtless it is satan's chosen instrument to ruin souls. After witnessing the ravages of intemperance for years in our country, and the efforts of the temperance societies and churches to suppress it, the total prohibition of the liquor traffic is now advocated by nearly all Christian churches and Christian workers. The largest denomination in the United States has declared that "The liquor traffic cannot be legalized without sin, and we proclaim as our motto, voluntary total abstinence from all intoxicants, as the true ground of personal temperance, and the complete legal prohibition of the traffic in intoxicating drinks, as the duty of civil governments. That no person engaged in the sale, or manufacture, of intoxicating liquors, for the purpose of their use as beverages, can be received in the church; and any person in the church who engages therein, subjects himself to disciplinary rebuke and punishment." When these Christian sentiments are embodied in the laws of the land, and the saloon is closed, then one of the greatest obstacles to the religious progress of our country will have been removed.

Perhaps the most common and popular habit, among male and female, in North Carolina is that of using tobacco in its different forms. When Walter Raleigh learned the use of tobacco, from the American Indians, and introduced it into England, little did he imagine that the Anglo Saxon race, as well as the other races of Europe, would take to the use of the weed as they have. But people were not satisfied with smoking it, and took to snuffing the powdered tobacco up their noses. How ridiculous the habit seems to us, now that the practice has ceased. It has been related that on one occasion the snuff-box was handed around in a little company, for each one to "take a pinch," and being offered to a kind of a wag of a fellow, he declined it saying, "No sir; if the Lord had intended my nose for a dust hole he would have put it on my face with the other end up." But the latest invention has transferred the snuff from the nose to the mouth, which is the "dust hole" now.

But is not the use of tobacco now an evil? Pehaps all who do not use it believe that it is, while many who do use it admit the evil of it. Some one in advocating the use of tobacco says that, "used in moderation it acts as a pleasing sedative." But who does use it in moderation? The general rule is, that the habit grows on those who use it, until they are in bondage to it, as are those who are addicted to opium and alcohol. Many claim that they cannot quit it, and if that is so, then tobacco has destroyed their will power, and their moral agency. This idea seems to be confirmed, in the fact that remedies are now advertised to cure the tobacco habit, taking it for granted that it is a disease, as is that of strong drink and opium. Here I have before me a popular and reliable newspaper with a full page of advertisement, headed "Don't tobacco smoke, and spit your life away," and offering "No-to-bac," as a remedy. The following statement is also made, and though it may not suit the popular taste, no doubt there is much sound sense in it. Nearly every day the newspapers give an account of some eminent man falling suddenly dead at his desk, from heart disease. As a rule, no middle-aged man in active business dies thus suddenly, unless poisoned, and that poison in a majority of cases is tobacco. Meanwhile the slaughter goes on. The press and the pulpit seem muzzled, the majority being participants in the popular vice, and those who are not, seem hypnotized, and afraid to speak out. The Cumberland Presbyterian General Assembly condemned the use of tobacco by a vote of 113 to 23; and the Reformed Presbyterian Synod has reaffirmed its action, forbidding any one to be licensed to preach who uses tobacco, and advises Sessions to appoint no Sunday School Superintendent who uses the weed.

Very recently the business manager of the St. Louis Christian Advocate made a visit to North Carolina, and writes up his visit here, giving some edifying facts in regard to the tobacco question. He says, "The devil knew very well that he could not come directly to the Anglo Saxon race with opium as he did with the Mongolian, hence he comes with tobacco, and through tobacco he reaches us with opium." Millions of people are wondering why it is they cannot and will not chew any other than the "Star Tobacco." It is the opium in this brand which is sapping the virtue and virility of its victims.

A few days ago we were in the manufactory of the most popular brand of smoking tobacco in the world, furnishing millions of victims on both sides of the sea. A large quantity of the ground tobacco is spread in a layer over a broad surface, over this, ground tonqua beans from South America are then spread. Over on this is then turned a large hose, through which a copious stream of unmitigated New England Rum is allowed to flow, until the whole mass is moistened. This then is packed in solid bales to go out into the mouths and membranes of the multitudes, decoying them like charmed birds unawares from rum in fumes to rum in liquids.

In the same city is a gigantic trust in the shape of a cigarette factory, yielding some of its stockholders hundreds of thousands of dollars annually, and paying its president a salary of fifty thousand dollars. With much reluctance we were once permitted to inspect the gambling iniquity of Monte Carlo. But this Carolina trust and iniquity, prohibits the entrance and inspection of visitors altogether. This restriction, they claim, is to protect their patents, but we have a lingering suspicion it is to protect their poisons.

But one of the most nauseating incongruities in the use of this weed, is where such a large number of young white women are seen with mops in their mouths dipping snuff. We were told of communities in North Carolina to which snuff is shipped by the car-load. What a wonderful field for lectures by the great hearted, brainy philanthropic women of our land. Put a text book on the physiological effects of alcohol and tobacco into the hands of each one of these girls, and let no Christian woman rest satisfied until every young woman in the South throws away her miserable mouth mop, and determines in soberness and cleanliness to breathe the balmy air of our blessed summer land." Having given above what this prominent Southern Methodist minister had to say of the tobacco question in North Carolina, I will say that he is only partially posted. He seems to think that a missionary to the young women of North Carolina is needed, and perhaps he would be surpised to know that a majority of the class he refers to are already professors of religion, and members of the different churches in our midst; and the snuff is not confined to the young women by any means, and the habit prevails among women of every age, and partially among the men also.

Perhaps the most ruinous effects of the use of tobacco are in the smoking of cigarettes, by our youngsters. Dr. Talmage says that "fifty young men in Brooklyn have died from cigarette smoking in a single winter." Here is a request for prayers sent in to one of the city prayer meetings: "Your prayers are asked for a boy of eighteen, of fine promise, but mentally diseased from cigarette smoking. Having escaped from an institution in which he was placed, he has for more than a month been wandering we know not where." Query. If cigarette smoking made an idiot of an eighteen-year old New York boy, how many North Carolina boys of eight or ten years, now smoking cigarettes, will be made idiots?

A Methodist lady not long since about Conference time said she hoped "that the preacher sent them would be one who did not use tobacco, for the sake of her boy, as she had taught him that it was wrong to use it."

The influence of the total abstainers from liquor and tobacco is no doubt counteracted by example of those of prominence and influence who claim to use these things in moderation. The following statement of a prominent minister in one of the Christian Advocates is to the point.

He says: "I had heard the Bishop address a class of young preachers, and among other advice urged them to forego or abandon the use of tobacco. I had myself but lately taken to smoking, but was so impressed with the Bishop's outlawry of the weed that I had made up my mind to abandon its use; I passed out of the Conference room, and lo! there sat Bishops Soule and Andrew on the steps of the parsonage pulling away on long-handled pipes, the very picture of contentment. All of my good intentions vanished into thin air at the sight."

I will give another illustrative incident on this point. Dr. Hamilton, a prominent minister, who had a perfect hatred of the pipe or cigar, was at a dining in company with a number of lawyers, statesmen, and ministers, and after dinner the host handed around Havanas, and proffered one to Dr. H., who drew himself up, saying, "No, sir, I'm a member of the Methodist Church, and a minister of the gospel." There was silence, and some inveterate smokers declined cigars, but the painful pause was broken by Bishop Soule, extending his withered hand to take one, and looking full at Dr. H., saying, "So am I, sir, and was before you were born." What would now be thought of a pair of bishops pipe smoking in a public place?

I will give an incident, the subject of which was one of our good old North Carolina preachers. He was a great smoker, and while he was at the house of one of his brethren, a youngster kept up a continual whistling, and at last, the preacher, being rather annoyed by it, by way of reproof said to him, "John, can you tell me which of the Apostles it was that whistled?" The answer was: "I don't know, sir, but I reckon it was the one that smoked."

This seems to be a day of imitations, and adulterations in almost every. thing, and from facts brought to light it appears that there are stronger motives than ever for a reformation in the use of tobacco, because of the mischievous drugs used in putting it up, and the more mischievous effects upon the health of those who use it.

The Wise man said that man was "made upright, but he has sought out many inventions," and a poet has said;

> "Since man by sin has lost his God,
> He seeks creation through,
> And vainly strives for solid bliss,
> In trying something new."

This disposition is manifested by idolaters in multiplying the number of false gods. The Athenians had twenty thousand idols, and desired yet another god, and so reared an altar to the

Unknown God. In this country, though the idols have no shape or form, yet many practice spiritual idolatry in rendering supreme regard or homage to other objects than the true God, these objects varying according to the ruling passion of the worshiper. First, there is the money god, or god of covetousness, for the Scriptures represent "covetousness as idolatry." This god is quite popular in our country, and those who worship him are taught to obtain worldly goods by many acts of fraud, and dishonesty, extortion, robbery, &c. There is a motto on our silver dollar, as most of us know, "In God we trust." Is not this a huge joke? Heathens who haven't seen one of these dollars, might suppose them to be simply images of the god we worship in this country.

Then there is the pleasure god, who dictates to his worshipers the different kinds of carnal enjoyment, such as licentiousness, and indulgence in popular amusements of the day. And near of kin to this is the fashion god. This god issues his orders from Paris and New York to his votaries, and the first lesson he teaches is, that "you had just as well be out of the world as out of the fashion." He fixes the standard of what is etiquette, style, and fashion in dress. All who conform to the demands of fashion in these things without regard to decency, economy or health, are worshipers of this god.

The Society woman who obeys the dictates of fashion, without regard to the laws of modesty and decency, as well as the precepts of the New Testament, proves that she is a worshiper of the fashion god, and is as truly an idolater as the woman of China or India who bows down to a visible image of her god. And in the land of idols there is the difference, the women there would not be allowed such an exposure of their persons before the public as is allowed in fashionable society in this Christian country. It is doubtful if the devil could invent anything more absurd and unnatural in the way of dress, than that of a woman with the upper part of her body entirely naked, and below her heels a yard or two of her dress goods dragging the ground.

An old lady friend of mine once told me that in her girl-hood days she saw a picture representing "Fashion, and the Devil." It showed Fashion as having hemmed him up in a corner picking at him, and teasing him to "just make her one more fashion," while the devil, being wearied out, replied, "O, I can't think of any more fashions."

The question of dress is a very simple one. The Apostle lays down the injunction in reference to women, in 1 Tim 1: 9, which requires them to observe the rule of *modesty*, *plainness*, and *economy*. A recent writer in one of the Church Advocates puts it thus: "We Christians punch holes in our ears, and dangle bangles on our wrists, and send out missionaries to tell the people, who are a century older than we, that they are heathens because they jingle bangles on their ankles, and hang jewels in their noses. What is the difference between barbarians who punch holes in their noses, and put in jewels, and those who punch holes in their ears, and put in jewels?"

Let society and worldly minded church members plead for the fashionable amusements of the day, in opposition to the teaching of the pulpit, but the fact remains that they are demoralizing in their tendency, and much more so than they were a generation ago. The old fashion farmhouse dance then was a decent thing compared to the fashionable dances of the present day; and the demoralization will go on among those who participate in them. The habits and customs of society in this day are certainly not favorable to female virtue. Let the record of those who have come to grief testify on this point.

In a preceding chapter some comments are made in regard to the unjust sentiment prevailing in society, which requires a higher standard of moral character in women than in men; and I am gratified to learn that since those lines were penned, a jurist of high position has expressed himself in sympathy with the sentiments of the writer. Judge Wilson, in behalf of his client in the great Breckinridge-Pollard suit, made a plea for women, and afterward declared his purpose "to use his influence in favor of establishing a moral and social code, that will visit upon the offending man the same measure of condemnation that it visits upon the offending woman." Now, Judge Wilson has struck the right chord, and let the good women act upon the suggestion, and organize for reform, requiring of men just what the men require of them, in order to receive them as associates. Let the women do this, for a reform along this line mainly depends on them.

Before closing these sketches I will present some thoughts in regard to the present surroundings in North Carolina. It is known that the country is passing through, if it will get through, one of the greatest financial depressions of the century, while there are four political parties now, each one presenting their theories as a remedy for existing evils, and on the eve of the election meeting in combat their political opponents; and however the present contest may result, it is questionable whether any political party, can or will remedy the evils which we suffer.

It is noticeable that more than one political orator, on visiting some towns to address the people, had to hold over on account of revivals of religion that were in progress, and may be it might be well to mix a little more religion with the politics of the day. To bring the country so under the influence of Christianity that people would practice the religion that Christ taught, would be the best way to remedy the Trusts and Monopolies, and to end the corner of the Pullmans, and all other oppressors of the people.

If any one wishes to know why there is such demoralization of society, while the gospel is preached so universally, and Sabbath School instruction is afforded to so many, let him take a glance at the secular newspapers of the day, and a number of them Sunday papers at that; then let him pass along through the principal streets of our cities and towns, and notice the character of the theatrical and circus advertisements, and other posters, and he can form some idea of the many "Schools of vice," outside of the church and Sabbath School, which will surely produce a crop of vicious men in due time. I will here specify, and comment a little.

A Sabbath or two ago I came up to the platform of a railroad station in one of our towns, and witnessed the scenes of Sabbath desecration there. Outside of the work carried on by the employees of the covetous Rail-road syndicate, on the arrival of the train, I noticed seven shoeblacks, five of them having a job of "shining" the shoes of the same number of white and colored "gentlemen," while the colored omnibus bosses were drumming up customers for the hotels. This is a specimen of the Sunday railroading in our Christian country.

Perhaps the secular newspapers may be named as one of the principal schools of vice, portraying as they do the scandals, immoralities and crimes occurring throughout the country, and placing these things in a sensational manner before the youth of our land.

Again, the glaring show bills of Peck's Bad Boy, facing the streets of our towns, indicate the fact that it is now being exhibited through the country; and will not the exhibition of this "Bad Boy," as a hero, tend to the demoralization of our boys, leading untold numbers of them to imitate him instead of a good boy? If so, then there is another school of vice.

Then there is a kind of mania prevailing for certain kinds of amusements which have become quite popular, which in itself is rather an indication of their doubtful propriety. Take for example the base-ball and foot-ball craze. It will not do to estimate the merits of it by the opinion of those who claim that it tends to muscular development, &c., while the game is so brutal as to endanger life and limbs. This very day I copied from a poster the following notice:

"FOOT-BALL CHAMPIONSHIP GAME,"
RICHMOND COLLEGE, VS. NORTH CAROLINA. GREENSBORO:" ADMISSION 50 CENTS.

By way of illustration I will quote from a prominent North Carolina newspaper, that sketches a recent contest between the University and Georgetown foot-ball teams. "When the referee had cleared away the debris, O'Brien's right cheek was badly cut. Guion and two others of his team had bloody noses, and nearly all of the players were spotted with their own or some one else's blood." Query; what is the difference between the morality of such a game as this, and the bull fights of Spain and Mexico?

Taking the above as a sample, let us analyze it in the light of Christianity. Leaving out the cost of the outfit for the game, and the shoe leather that is *kicked* out, consider the actual money involved in it. First, estimate the amount of rail-road fare required to transport these teams from one city to another, and add to it the fifty cents for each individual of the crowds that go to see the sport. Then consider, that while every man is a steward of God, and accountable to him for the use of his money, all of this money is worse than wasted, while millions of our race are in the darkness of heathenism, and men are ready to go as missionaries, but the church has not money to send them; and money is needed also for other benevolent causes at home. And in view of the fact that the apostle has laid upon us the injunction that, "whether we eat or drink, or whatsoever we do," we are to "do all to the glory of God," let each individual man, and especially every professing Christian, who engages in these sports, inquire if the divine sentence is not applicable to them, "Thou art weighed in the balances, and art found wanting?"

As the reader will see, I have chosen to refer to myself as *I*, and not *we*, as is the editorial style of many writers; and as these sketches contain some autobiography, and a number of incidents in which I was a prominent actor, I have necessarily used the personal pronoun pretty often, yet I hope my writing does not contain so many big I's that the printer will be put to it to find enough of them to set up in type my manuscript.

. In my autobiographical sketches I have not

gone back far enough to take in my boyhood pranks. If I had done so, perhaps the reader would have concluded that I did not belong to that class of young ones that were so good they didn't live, and were taken away out of this sinful world, but would regard me rather as a specimen of Peck's Bad Boy, and as I have advanced the idea in the preceding pages that such things have a demoralizing tendency, I have not gone so far back in my individual career.

In concluding these sketches I may say, that perhaps the views I have expressed in regard to some moral questions may not be in agreement with the ideas of some, and may invoke criticism; and I will give an illustrative incident, and make an application. A prominent minister was preaching a doctrinal sermon, and he advanced an idea that was not in agreement with the creed of an old lady who sat before him, and she showed her dissent by an audible *grunt*. The preacher went on, and when he advanced another idea in the same line she gave a louder *grunt*, and all this time the preacher held his peace, but when for the third time the old lady gave a still louder *grunt*, the preacher paused, and pointing his finger straight at the offender, he said, "Sister, *did I hurt you?*" Now, as to the application: If any of my readers, on reading anything I have written, should give a grunt, I will say, did I hurt you? Or in other words, did I *hit* you?

And now, being conscious that my writing, upon the whole, has been in the interest of truth, and in the light of the Holy Scriptures, I "commend it to every man's conscience in the sight of God."

APPENDIX.

Note.—When the preceding sketches were commenced, the idea of adding an Appendix had not been entertained, but was an after-thought. The subject certainly is an important one, involving the destiny of our country. I have no apology to offer any one, not even the despot at Rome.

CHAPTER I.

The Romish hierarchy identified as the great Anti-Christ of Revelation—The whole system shown from the Scriptures to be false—Its intolerance and persecutions.

A PROMINENT religious journal recently quoted a noted Protestant D. D. as saying, that if we should attack Romanism it might give Romanists occasion to say that they were being persecuted; and he condemned the idea of "fighting the devil with fire." But I beg leave to dissent from the Rev. Doctor. As "the devil is a liar, and the father of lies," we may surely fight his lies with the weapon of God's truth. Christianity embraces aggressive warfare, and as I believe that Romanism embraces the "doctrines of devils," I feel as much authorized to attack it as I would any other machinery the devil has put in operation to deceive and mislead mankind. Luther, Calvin, Knox, and other reformers fought it, and we may do the same wherever it may exist. And especially is it timely to do so now, while these enemies of our country and of our Protestant Christianity, are working in the dark to undermine our institutions.

Romanism claims for the pope universal dominion, and that he has authority given him from heaven over all ecclesiastical and civil powers. It is professedly intolerant, and persecution, as a matter of course, follows, and wherever it dominates, punishes as heretics those who refuse to receive its dogmas. And mark it, what Romanism has done in other countries, it will do here, in our country, when it can get control of the secular power.

Now I invite the reader to follow me, Bible in hand, in my exposition of the Scriptures, identifying the papacy as the great Anti-Christ. St. John in his vision, recorded in the 17th chapter of Revelation, "Saw a woman sitting on a scarlet colored beast, whose name was called 'mystery,' Babylon the great, the mother of Harlots, and abominations of the earth ; and mark it, that the angel who showed John these things, in explanation of the vision, stated that the woman "was that great city which reigneth over the kings of the earth." See verse 18. What city did reign supreme, at that day ? Answer, Rome, which was called the mistress of the world. 2 That the seven heads of the beast were "seven mountains on which the woman sitteth." See verse 9. Rome was built on seven hills, and was called "the seven-hilled city." This fixes the seat of the beast at Rome, which has ever been the seat of the papacy. 3 The beast "was full of names of blasphemy." See verse 3. Here mark the blasphemous titles of Romanism. "My Lord God the pope, and Mary mother of God and Queen of heaven" &c. 4 The beast was "scarlet colored," and "the woman was arrayed in purple, and scarlet color." See verse 3. Is not the favorite color of the Romish dignitaries designated here? Whenever a cardinal makes his appearance look out for the "scarlet cap," 5 The woman was "drunken with the blood of the saints, and the martyrs of Jesus." See verse 6. Here is indicated persecution and blood-shed by the woman, which has been fulfilled in the history of the Romish Church. See "Fox's Book of martyrs," and the history of the Reformation. In the "Massacre of St. Bartholomew" at least 80,000 Huguenots were slain; and according to the record before me, there were put to death from 1481 to 1783 in Spain, under the different cardinals, arch-bishops, bishops and inquisitors 23,802 men and women. Besides these, there were put to death under the secular power, guided by papal Rome, no less than 36,656, making a total of 60,458. These do not include the thousands put to death under the famous inquisition. If the blood of all these was not sufficient to make the woman "drunken," how much blood would it take?

I will cite some other scriptures as testimony in the same line. In Paul's 1st epistle to Timothy, he states that in the departure from the faith, some would "give heed to seducing spirits and doctrines of devils," and designates "forbidding to marry" as one of them. This is fulfilled in the Romish Church, which forbids the priests to marry. See 1 Tim. 4: 1 3. Again, in 2 Thess. 2: 3, &c, "the man of sin" is represented as "sitting in the temple of God and showing himself that he is God." In the fulfillment of this scripture mark that the pope, sitting in the temple of God, claims universal dominion, and is declared to be infallible; and in the Romish canon law it is stated that he was called God, by the pious Constantine, and he is also called "Our Lord," by the Romish dignitaries.

I will refer to 1 Tim. 4: 2. where apostates from the faith are represented as "speaking lies in hypocrisy," &c., and will point out some of the hypocritical lies, embraced in the Romish dogmas. 1 That Peter was the first pope, and that the pope of Rome is his successor. This is entirely unscriptural, and false, for Peter never claimed, or attempted to exercise, any authority over any of the rest of the apostles, claiming to be only an Elder in the Church, among the other elders. See 1 Pet. 5: 1, &c. On the contrary, on one occasion Paul rebuked Peter, and Peter certainly never issued any Pope's bull against him for it either. See Gal. 2: 11, &c. The fact is, no higher order of the ministry was recognized in the Apostolic Church, than that of bishop or elder. And how dare any man to call himself a pope, a cardinal or arch-bishop, and "lord it over God's heritage." As to Peter being the "head of the Church," as Romanists claim; what a ridiculous sight it would be to see a man's body with another man's head on it. So it is a most absurd idea to think of any mortal man being the head of "Christs body, which is the Church."

2 The dogma of auricular confession, requiring confession of sin to a priest, in order to receive forgiveness, making the priest the medium of access to God, instead of Christ. In fact, since Christ, our "One Mediator between God and man," and our "Great High Priest," came and made his one offering, and "ascended up on high, ever living to make intercession for us," no man has any right to assume the office of a priest; and so confession to a priest has no foundation in the scriptures.

3 Praying to the Virgin Mary, and paying her divine honors, as the mother of God, &c., while neither Christ or the apostles ever intimated that we should make prayer to any besides "Our Father who art in heaven." Roman Catholics

pray to other dead saints also, and also offer prayers for the dead.

4 Purgatory, represented as the half-way place between heaven and hell, where, they say, souls are detained, until the priest offers prayers to get them out. While this has not a vestige of scriptural authority, it is a source of great revenue to the priests, and not only do living Catholics pay for masses for the souls of their dead friends, but some, when they die, leave money to be appropriated to paying for masses to be said for the repose of their souls.

5 Transubstantiation, or the pretended changing of the bread and wine, in the Lord's Supper, into the real body and blood of Christ, and the idea is assumed that thereby the priest offers continually the body of Christ, as a Sacrifice. Reader, did you ever witness the Romish ceremony of "elevating the host?" On certain occasions, after going through the ceremony of making Christ out of a cake of bread, the priest takes the cake, on the end of a rod or spear, and from the altar, lifts it upon high above the heads of the congregation, when they all bow down and worship that cake of bread!

Besides these, there are other dogmas, or sacraments, as they call them, such as penance, extreme unction, and indulgences, or the pardon of sin before it is committed ; in other words, the selling of permits to commit sin. If any one wishes to know the merits of this thing let them read an account of the times of Luther, when that grand humbug Tetzel peddled indulgences all over the country. It may be said that in this enlightened day, and in this country, Romanism could never be what it was in the old world, but wherever it prevails it will be practiced. It has proven a curse to every country where it has dominated, as in Italy, Ireland, Spain, and Mexico, where ignorance, superstition, and social degradation prevail. "Priest-ridden" is a significant term to express the condition of those under the rule of Romanism, which tends to the impoverishment of the people, while it enriches the priests.

In order to show what Romanism really is, I will quote from their canon law, and also give the oaths which are taken by cardinals, bishops, priests, and those who join the Secret order of Jesuits. "Canon law section 9. That the pontiff was called God. by the pious Constantine, and that as God he cannot be judged as man." Section 10. "That as God he is far above the reach of all human law, and judgment." Section 15. "The civil law is derived from man, but the ecclesiastical or canon law is derived directly from God, by which the pontiff can, in connection with his prelates, make constitutions for the whole Christian world, in matters spiritual, concerning the salvation of souls, and the right government of the church; and if necessary judge, and dispose of all the temporal goods of all Christians." Section 18. "The goods of heretics are to be confiscated, and applied to the Church." Section 20. "The secular powers, whether permanent or temporary, are bound to swear that they will exterminate, according to their power, all heretics condemned by the church;" and a temporal lord not purging his land of heretics, is excommunicated. Section 27. "No oath is to be kept toward heretics, princes, lords, or others." Section 31. "The pope can absolve from all oaths."

CARDINAL'S OATH—"I,———, cardinal of the Holy Roman church, do promise and swear that, from this time to the end of my life, I will be faithful and obedient unto St. Peter, the holy apostolic Roman church, and our most holy lord, the pope of Rome and his successors, canonically and lawfully elected: that I will give no advice, consent or assistance against the pontificial majesty and person; that I will never knowingly and advisedly, to their injury or disgrace, make public the councils entrusted to me by themselves, or by messengers or letters; also that I will give them any assistance in retaining, defending and recovering the Roman papacy and the regalia of Peter, with all my might and endeavor, so far as the rights and privileges of my order will allow it, and will defend them against all their honor and state, and I will direct and defend, with due form and honor, the legates and nuncios of the apostolic see, in the territories, churches, monasteries and other benefices committed to my keeping; and I will cordially co-operate with them and treat them with honor in their coming, abiding and returning, and that I will resist unto blood all persons whatsoever who shall attempt anything against them. That I will, by every way and by every means strive to preserve, augment and advance the rights, honors, privileges, the authority of the Holy Roman bishop, our lord the pope and his before mentioned successors, and that, at whatever time anything shall be decided to their prejudice, which is out of my power to hinder, as soon as I shall know that any steps or measures have been taken in the matter, I will make it known to the same, our lord or his successors, or some other person by whose means it may be brought to their knowledge. That I will keep and carry out and cause others to keep and carry out the rules of the holy father, the decrees, ordinaces, dispensations, reservations, provisions, apostolic mandates and constitutions of the Holy Father Sextus, of happy memory, as to visiting the thresholds of the apostles at certain prescribed times, according to the tenor of that which I have just read through. That I will seek out and oppose, persecute and fight against heretics or schismatics who oppose our lord, the pope of Rome, and his before-mentioned successors, and this I will do with every possible effort."

‡ (Signature) then sent to the pope.

BISHOP'S OATH.—"I, ———, ——— elect of the ———diocese, from henceforward will be faithful and obedient to St. Peter the Apostle and to the Holy Roman church, and to our lord, the holy pope of Rome, and to his successors, canonically entering, I will neither advise, consent nor do anything that they may lose life or member, or that their persons may be seized, or hands in anywise laid upon them, or any injuries offered to them, under any pretence whatsoever. The counsel with which they shall entrust me by themselves, their messengers or letters, I will not knowingly reveal to any, to their prejudice. I will help them to defend and keep the Roman papacy and the royalties of St. Peter against all men. The legate of the apostolic see, going and coming, I will honorably treat and help in his necessities. The rights, honors, privileges and authority of the Holy Roman church of our lord, the pope, and his aforesaid successors, I will endeavor to preserve, defend, increase and advance. I will not be in any counsel, action or treaty, in which shall be plotted against our said lord and Roman church, anything to the hurt or prejudice of their persons, rights, honor, state or power, and, if I shall know any such thing to be treated or agitated by any whatsoever, I will hinder it to my utmost, and as soon as I can, I will signify it to our lord. The ordinance and mandates of the pope, I will observe with all my might, and cause to be observed by others.

"Heretics, schismatics and rebels to our said lord or his successors, I will to my utmost persecute and oppose."

I will come to a council when I am called. I will visit the thresholds of the apostles every three years and give an account to our lord of all my pastoral office and of all the things belonging to my diocese, to the discipline of my clergy and people. I will in like manner humbly receive and diligently execute the apostolic commands. If I am detained by a lawful impediment, I will perform the aforesaid by a member of my chapter or a priest of my diocese, fully instructed in all things above mentioned. The possessions belonging to my table, I will neither sell nor otherwise alienate without consulting the Roman pontiff. So help me God and these holy gospels of God." (Signature) Sent to the Romish Manager.

PRIEST'S OATH.—"I——— ———,now in the presence of Almighty God, the blessed Virgin Mary, the blessed Michael the Archangel, the blessed St. John the Baptist, the Holy Apostles St. Peter and St. Paul and the Saints and the Sacred Hosts of Heaven and to you, my lord, I do declare from my heart, without mental reservation, that the pope is Christ's vicar-general and is the true and only head of the universal church throughout the earth, and that, by virtue of the keys of binding and loosing given to his holiness by Jesus Christ, he has power to depose heretical kings, princes, states, commonwealths and governments, all being illegal without his sacred confirmation, and that they may safely be destroyed. Therefore to the utmost of my power, I will defend this doctrine and his holiness' rights and custom against all usurpers of the Protestant authority whatsoever, especially against the now pretended authority and church in England and all adherents, in regard that they be usurpal and heretical, opposing the sacred mother of the church of Rome.

"I do denounce and disown any allegiance as due to any Protestant king, prince or state or obedience to any of their inferior officers. I do further declare the doctrine of the church of England, of the Calvinists, Huguenots and other Protestants, to be damnable and those to be damned who will not forsake the same.

"I do further declare that I will help, assist and advise all or any of his holiness' agents in any place wherever I shall be, and to do my utmost to extirpate the Protestant doctrine and to destroy all their pretended power, regal or otherwise. I do further promise and declare that, notwithstanding I may be permitted by dispensation to assume any heretical religion (Protestant denominations) for the propagation of the mother church's interest, to keep secret and private all her agents' counsels as they entrust me, and not to divulge, directly or indirectly, by word, writing or circumstances whatsoever, but to execute all which shall be proposed, given in charge or discovered unto me by you, my most reverend lord and bishop.

"All of which I,————, do swear by the blessed Trinity and blessed Sacrament which I am about to receive, to perform on my part to keep inviolably; and do call on all the Heavenly and Glorious Host of Heaven to witness my real intentions to keep this my oath.

"In testimony whereof I take this most holy and

blessed Sacrament of the Eucharist, and witness the same further with my consecrated hand, in the presence of my holy bishop and all the priests who assist him in my ordination to the priesthood."

EXTREME OATH OF THE JESUIT.—I, ———,
now in the presence of Almighty God, the blessed Virgin Mary, the blessed Michael the archangel, the blessed St. John the Baptist, the holy Apostles St. Peter and St. Paul and the saints and sacred hosts of heaven, and to you my ghostly father, the superior general of the society of Jesus, founded by Saint Ignatius Loyola in the pontification of Paul the Third, and continued to the present, do, by the womb of the virgin, the matrix of God, and the rod of Jesus Christ declare and swear that his holiness, the pope, is Christ's vicegerent, and is the true and only head of the Catholic or universal church throughout the earth; and that by virtue of the keys of binding and loosing given to his holiness by my Savior, Jesus Christ, he hath power to depose heretical kings, princes, states, commonwealths and governments, all being illegal without his sacred confirmation, and they may be safely destroyed. Therefore to the utmost of my power, I will defend this doctrine and his holiness' right and custom against all usurpers of the heretical or

Protestant authority whatsoever, especially the Lutheran church of Germany, Holland, Denmark, Sweden and Norway, and the now pretended authorities and churches of England and Scotland, and branches of the same now established in Ireland, and on the continent of America, and elsewhere, and all adherents in regard that they be usurped and heretical, opposing the sacred church of Rome.

I do now denounce and disown any allegiance as due to any heretical king, prince or state named Protestant or Liberals or obedience to any of their laws, magistrates or officers.

I do further declare that the doctrine of the churches of England and Scotland, of the Calvinists, Huguenots and others of the name of Protestants or Liberals to be damnable, and they themselves to be damned who will not forsake the same.

I do further declare that I will help, assist and advise all or any of his holiness' agents in any place wherever I shall be, in Switzerland, Germany, Holland, Denmark, Sweden, Norway, England, Iceland or America, or in any other kingdom or territory, I shall come to, and do my utmost to extirpate the heretical Protestant or Liberal doctrines, and to destroy all their pretended powers, legal or otherwise.

I do further promise and declare that, notwithstanding I am dispensed with to assume any religion heretical for the propagation of the mother church's interest, to keep secret and private all her agents' councils from time to time, as they entrust me, and not to divulge, directly or indirectly, by word, writing or circumstances whatever, but to execute all that shall be proposed, given in charge, or discovered unto me, by you or my ghostly father, or any of this sacred convent.

I do further promise and declare that I will have no opinion or will of my own or any mental reservation whatsoever, even as a corpse or cadaver (perinde ac cadaver), but will unhesitatingly obey each and every command that I may receive from my superiors in the militia of the pope and of Jesus Christ.

That I will go to any part of the world whithersoever I may be sent, to the frozen regions of the north, the burning sands of the desert of Africa, or the jungles of India, the centers of civilization of Europe, or to the wild haunts of the barbarous savages of America, without murmuring or repining, and will be submissive in all things whatsoever, communicated to me.

I do furthermore promise and declare that I will, when opportunity presents, make and wage relentless war, secretly or openly, against all heretics, Protestants and Liberals as I am directed to do, to extirpate them from the face of the whole earth, and that I will spare neither age, sex or condition, and that I will hang, burn, waste, boil, flay, strangle and bury alive these infamous heretics; rip up the stomachs of their women and crush their infants' heads against the walls in order to annihilate their execrable race. That when the same cannot be done openly, I will secretly use the poisonous cup, the strangulating cord, the steel of the poinard, or the leaden bullet, regardless of the honor, rank, dignity or authority of the person or persons, whatever may be their condition in life, either public or private, as I at any time may be directed so to do by any agent of the pope or superior of the brotherhood of the holy father, of the society of Jesus.

In confirmation of which I hereby dedicate my life, my soul and all corporal powers, and with this dagger which I now receive, I will subscribe my name, written in my blood, in testimony thereof; and should I prove false or weaken in my determination, may my brethren and fellow soldiers of the militia of the pope cut off my hands and my feet, and my throat from ear to ear, my belly opened and sulphur burned therein, with all the punishment that can be inflicted upon me on earth and my soul be tortured by demons in an eternal hell forever.

All of which I,......................, do swear by the blessed trinity, and blessed sacrament which I am now to receive, to perform, and on my part to keep inviolably; and do call all the heavenly and glorious host of heaven to witness these, my real intentions, to keep this my oath.

In testimony hereof I take this most holy and blessed sacrament of the eucharist, and witness the same further, with my name written with the point of this dagger, dipped in my own blood, and seal in the face of this holy convent.

[He receives the wafer from the superior and writes his name with the point of his dagger, dipped in his own blood, taken from over the heart.]

The following from a recent writer is to the point.

"JESUITISM OUR GREAT DANGER."

"The Society of Jesuits, one of the most celebrated orders of the Roman Catholic Church, was founded by Ignatius Loyola in 1540. The reigning pope Paul 3 immediately, by his bull, sanctioned the institution. These minions of the papacy, are the sworn enemies of every government save that of the pope only, and that to effect the objects of their order they will not hesitate to profess any Protestant or heathen faith under the sun. They will obtrude themselves into public schools as teachers, and upon the rostrum as lecturers and preachers, assuming for the occasion a sacerdotal, or a citizen's garb. The United States is the fruitful field for the Jesuits. Already they control all the principal cities of the country. They have organized many Roman Catholic military societies, ostensibly as United States militia, and they are officered by some of the most skillful generals of the country. And what constitutes the greatest source of danger to the country is, that Protestants look upon the growing power of the papacy with stolid indifference."

And while these Jesuits have been expelled from Italy, Germany, and France, and other countries of Europe, and lately from Mexico, they are allowed full liberty here in our country, by the United States government.

As the Romish system is false and corrupt in principle, it must be also corrupt in its administration, and its administrators. Let no one be deceived by the pious cant, and holy phrases, paraded before the public, such as "Vicar of Christ, Successor of St. Peter," and "His holiness," as applied to the pope, and "holy Father" as applied to "bachelor priests."

History testifies to the crimes of Romanism.

Take for example the inquisition or eclesiastical court, established to try, and punish heretics, which they call all who dissent from the Romish dogmas. When Napoleon marched his army into Spain he unearthed the secret chamber of the inquisition, and there found their machinery for torturing heretics.

I will quote from a recent writer, showing what the inquisition was at Rome in 1849, when the revolution took place, and the pope fled from his palace. "The doors of the inquisition were unlocked, and its hideous secrets exposed. The gloomy building stood close to St. Peter's Church. Through double folding gates of brass, was the passage into a large court, surrounded by buildings set apart for the use of the inquisition. These contained prisons, with cells hardly large enough to contain one person. In each cell was an enormous iron ring, made to open and close with a padlock. This ring was fixed either to the wall or to the stone floor, and was intended to encircle the body of the prisoner. The walls were covered with inscriptions, in all languages. Some of these were dictated by grief and despair, others bore the impression of resignation. One prisoner wrote. "The caprice or wickedness of man cannot exclude me from thy Church, O Christ." Another wrote, "how much have I suffered here." Another wrote, "I am innocent; I am accused of not being a Catholic, but I believe in the Father, Son and Holy Ghost." Another wrote, "Blessed are they who are persecuted for righteousness' sake, for theirs is the kingdom of heaven." Another wrote in his bodily anguish; "The Lord is my shepherd, I shall not want." And may we not to-day, as it were, add our inscription. "The noble army of martyrs praise thee."

In the midst of the dungeons, was the torture chamber, a large vaulted hall of stone. Here up to 1815 had been the rack to draw the joints asunder, the pully to crack the sinews, the hissing pincers to tear the quivering flesh from the bones, the brazier filled with burning charcoal, to roast the feet. Here had the Romish inquisition sat unmoved, listening to the groans of the tortured ones, viewing their convulsive pangs, and turning a deaf ear to the piteous cry for mercy. There is an awfully solemn future when, as we learn from scripture, God himself will make *inquisition* for blood, and when he will say, speaking of Rome: "Reward her even as she rewarded you, and double unto her double, according to her works—in the cup which she hath filled, fill to her double * * * torment and sorrow, give her. See Rev., 18: 6.

As to the priesthood, and monastic institutions, St. Paul said, "A bishop must be the husband of one wife," and characterizes "forbidding to marry," as one of the "doctrines of devils." And he also said, "I will that the young women marry," and as Romish priests are forbidden to marry, and young girls are brought under their influence in the confessional, those outside, as well as inside of the convents, the result has been, and no doubt will continue to be, that scandalous sins and inmoralities will continue to proceed from the confessional and the convents. It is asserted that in Den's and Kenrick's Theology, the priests are instructed to ask young girls, in the confessional, the most demoralizing questions. If any one denies this, he is challenged to produce the books, and disprove the statement.

Let us take a view of the monastic system in the light of the scriptures. Christ characterized his disciples as the "light of the world," and as "a city that is set on a hill," and how can any one fulfill his injunction, "Let your light so shine before men," by withdrawing from the world, and secluding himself or herself in the recesses of a monastery, or convent. Young girls are decoyed into taking vows, and entering a convent by flattering representations of the life of a nun and after they enter there many realize it to be a prison, and among their keepers, bachelor priests. Let the number of "escaped nuns" who have given their experience of convent life testify. It pays to persuade young girls to take the veil, and enter a convent, who are heiresses, as one of their vows, as a nun is *poverty*, and then their money is turned over to the holy Fathers. The following clippings from recent publications are much to the point.

—CLOSED CONVENTS SHOULD NOT BE TOLERATED IN A FREE COUNTRY.—Every convent in this land is a blotch on our soil, a reproach on our institutions. They are tombs of the living, not of the dead. The man who assists in the ceremony of burying a young heart in one of these frightful holes commits a crime against humanity. We burn with hot indignation at the picture! The world's pity should go with the poor, deluded being who offers up her young heart, its great lovings and cravings unknown to herself, and goes with her priest to a willing dungeon—to a fate which is as dark as night, but after she has been there a year the world's justice should go and find out if she wishes to escape from her jailor. If there is in this land a house not under lawful supervision which an inmate cannot leave when she wishes to, the doors of that house should be opened by the hand of the law or its walls torn down.

We have been moved to write the above by reading the account of the escape of a girl seventeen years old from St. Ann's Home in New York City. The girl risked her life to escape from the place, which had become intolerable to her. She made a rope of sheets and blankets and lowered herself to the ground from an upper window.

Why should we allow ecclesiastics to keep young women shut up in houses against their will? If these persons are criminals, then the state should care for them; if they are not, it is a crime to deprive them of liberty and should be punished severely. Too many cases like this come under our eye not to take notice of them. Our country is disgraced by every convent on its soil. It is time they were abolished by law.

If the Roman Catholic church wishes to establish houses for aged women who are homeless, friendless, tired of life's struggles and sick of its vices and its wrongs, let it do so, but there is no charity in building houses in which to imprison young, handsome and talented women, who are allowed to see no man but a priest, and who pass their lives in doing—no one outside of the convent walls knows what. We do not believe that a convent would ever be built if priests were excluded from their doors.

When the Italian convents were opened to the world by Garabaldi, all doubts as to the statements of ex-nuns and ex-priests must have been swept away. Indisputable evidence upon indisputable evidence has been added, until it is proved beyond the shadow of a doubt that the grossest immorality exists behind the bolted and barred doors of those so called holy edifices.

It is a notorious fact that popes have been charged with the grossest crimes. Abbott in his history of Christianity says that the leading cardinals, arch-bishops, and bishops appointed by infamous popes and kings, were almost universally irrelegious and corrupt men."

The Empeor Maximilian wrote to one of the leading men in the Saxon court, "All the popes I have had anything to do with, have been rogues and cheats."

And as to the character of the monastic institutions in Europe, Lyman Abbott in his Dictionary of Religious knowledge says, "they had become the hot-beds of profligacy, and vice." There was an attempt at reforming the monasteries, but "the begging monks wandered over all Europe, and they covered the country like swarms of locusts," proclaiming everywhere, the obedience due to the holy mother church, the reverence to the saints,—and more especially to the Virgin Mary—the efficacy of relics, the torments of purgatory, and the blessed advantage arising from indulgences. The profligacy and deep-seated corruption of the monastic institutions, had now reached its height; and at this point in the history of monachism the Reformation burst upon the world." See Dictionary of Religious Knowledge, under the head of Monachism.

And since the Reformation, where Romanism has ruled, how much better are these monastic institutions? When Napoleon raided the convents and monasteries of Europe, he found evidences enough of the hidden corruptions within, even murder, and infanticide. The enforced celibacy of the priests, the confessional, and the monastic system being unscriptural and false, will always, and everywhere, produce licentiousness, and scandalous immoralities. I have the record before me of a number of such cases of recent occurrence, in the United States, involving Catholic priests and the convents, but which I will withhold, for the reason that it would make the reading matter not decent enough for my Christian readers.

Here I will call to mind a historical fact, which most persons will remember, that a very few years ago, the Catholic priest at Raleigh, N. C., was sentenced to be hanged for a brutal assault on a young lady, the daughter of one of his flock. In the language of a recent writer, "Let a cry go up from the American people, and let their voices be heard, demanding an open investigation of all Roman convents."

There are in the United States, according to Abbott's Dictionary of Religious Knowledge, published in 1875, 300 nunneries, and 128 monasteries, besides 112 schools for the education of girls, and 400 for the education of boys; and this is believed to be far below the real number, as there is a disposition to conceal the actual work done; and while the term monk and nun no longer appear very often in the Roman Catholic organs, monastic orders are as active and efficient as they ever were. The arch-diocese of Baltimore alone contains 21 convents, in all of which education is carried on.

And what do they teach in these schools? Here I will give some specimens of the Catechetical instruction imparted to the young, with the approbation of the arch-bishop of Baltimore. "No salvation outside of the Roman Catholic church." Lesson 12. Question. "Since the Roman Catholic alone is the true church of Jesus, can any one who dies outside of the church be saved?

Answer. He cannot." Question. "Did Jesus Christ himself assure us most solemnly, and in plain words, that no one can be saved out of the Roman Catholic Church? Answer. He did, when he said to his Apostles, go and teach all nations," &c. Question. "Are there any other reasons to show that heretics or Protestants, who die out of the Roman Catholic Church, are not saved? Answer, there are several. They cannot be saved, because, 1 They have no divine faith. 2. They make a liar of Jesus Christ, of the Holy Ghost, and of the Apostles. 3. They have no faith in Christ. 4. They fell away from the true church of Christ. 5. They are too proud to submit to the pope, the Vicar of Christ. 6. They cannot perform any good works, whereby they can obtain heaven. 7. They do not receive the body and blood of Christ. 8. They die in their sins. 9. They ridicule and blaspheme the mother of God, and his saints. 10. They slander the spouse of Jesus, the Catholic church."

CHAPTER II.

Romanism in our own country—More light turned on the subject—The pope in our politics—No real Catholic can be a true citizen of our Republic—Some historical facts showing the influence of Romanism over the United States Government.

IN order to understand the real policy of the Romish church, and her designs towards our country, I will give here the private instructions of the priests to the Catholic people in the United States.

TO OUR BELOVED CHILDREN IN THE FAITH:— In view of the pressing necessity for active, earnest efforts on the part of all Catholics to save our holy church from destruction; to preserve the income and privileges which we of the hierarchy have enjoyed for a thousand years; to maintain the absolute supremacy which is ours by divine right: the pleasure of shriving the masses who have toiled and economized, that we might live in peace and holy contentment; to continue to build fine churches and cathedrals as mural monuments to perpetuate our faith; to preserve ignorance in the masses, and thus insure devotion; to enable us to keep our vows of celibacy, with the aid of the confessional; to prevent the loss of prestige and political power; it becomes necessary for the hierarchy of the holy church, in these infidel parts, called the United States, that we may carry out the orders contained in an encyclical letter from Pope Leo XIII., our holy father, that we organize a political party to be known as the Catholic party. and that the faithful may not be ignorant of their duties as voters under this heretical government, we here announce and publish the following platform and principles, or more properly,

ORDERS FROM THE HOLY SEE.

Whereas, many Catholics in the United States have become careless in the discharge of their religious duties, more especially in elections, it becomes our duty to call your attention to the orders of the holy father, as expressed by Pius IX., of holy memory, in a letter dated December, 1864—also to another letter dated January, 1890, by Leo XIII. In these two encyclical letters you have the voice of God speaking to you, and with pain and sorrow we are by duty to God and our holy father, constrained to remind you of your duty to your faith when you vote as a citizen of this heretical nation.

We also call your attention to the words of your bishops from time to time, the holy fathers to whom you must look for direction in the affairs of your lives. What they direct you to do, you must do, if you hope for the salvation which our holy church alone can give. These holy men have frequently counseled you and commanded you to do many things which you have not done, hence we issue this manifesto to instruct you as to your duty to your religion when you vote.

It is our desire that in future you cease to act as Democrats or Republicans, only so far as is necessary to secure election to office, or aid in the election of one who when elected will serve only our holy church. You must never forget that you are Catholics, that your first and constant allegiance is to our holy father in Rome, and that this allegiance takes precedence over all others, and necessitates that all your acts, political or otherwise, must be conducted solely with reference to the supremacy of our holy father as the supreme spiritual and temporal ruler of the world. Let your votes be cast as loyal sons of our holy church, and not as loyal to this heretical usurpation which has merited and received the major excommunication of our former holy father Pius IX., of holy memory. We enjoin all pastors throughout that part of the western hemisphere called the United States, and mentioned by the holy college as [infidel parts,] that they read these instructions to their congregations for four successive Sundays at every mass, and in the sermon explain and enforce them upon the attention and understanding of the faithful, and above all, to see that the line of duty deemed necessary by the holy father be strictly enforced, or that the disobedient be denied the sacraments of our holy church, failing that, they will be subjected to the "Major excommunication."

We view with alarm the rapid spread of American education, knowing full well that wherever the people are intelligent, the priest and prince cannot hope to have the same unquestioning obedience as from the masses whose brains have been fertilized only with our holy catechism. That in order to restore the order of things that made the reign of Gregory VII., of holy memory, so glorious, the people must not *think*, that is a privilege that belongs only to priests and princes, who by divine right, are the only persons designated by God to do the political and religious thinking of this world.

We view with alarm the rapid diffusion of the English language. It stands before the world as the tongue which has for three hundred years ever been opposed to our holy church; those who speak it have been foremost in assailing the holy see. It is the tongue in which heresy delights to annoy and refute our theologians, in which the modern damnable heresies of popular rule, government of the people, equal rights, personal liberty, free thought, free press, free religion and free schools, find expression, and endanger the rights of the hierarchy, and also that of princes born to rule.

We view with alarm and horror the indifference exhibited by the states of the civilized world when they behold the sacrilege and impiety of the Italians, in taking by force from the holy father his temporal possessions, thus depriving him of the ability to levy taxes from the people of the papal states, also robbing him of the glory which was proper and necessary for the ruler over three million subjects. We must all pledge ourselves to never rest until the holy father is restored to his temporal throne, and those who have perpetrated this robbery be adequately punished.

We view with alarm and apprehension the growth of numerous American orders or societies in this land. It is to us evidence that our measures for quieting the American people were insufficient, that we have been too bold, did not exercise that wisdom that many centuries of experience should have given us. We learn that these societies will not vote for candidates of our faith, or even those who are friendly to us, hence it becomes our duty to take measures to thwart this uprising, which may result in our utter discomfiture. We therefore condemn, in strong terms, this aggregation of heretics in secret societies, and call on our faithful brothers of the Society of Jesus, to send members of that holy brotherhood into these societies to get their rituals and other secrets, that we may print them in the daily papers that do our bidding, and thus expose them, that they may be shunned by the faithful, and injured in their business, reputations or families. We also call on the clergy everywhere to organize the laity, male and female, old and young, into secret societies and sodalities, and that the men and boys may have competent instructors to give them military training that they may be prepared to aid and sustain our faith in an emergency.

That the faithful may fully understand their duty when they act in accordance with this platform, we here announce the laws, which every lay member of our holy communion is bound to obey, or be deprived of the holy sacraments of his faith:

1. The holy father is the supreme ruler of the world, more especially in temporal matters where we have the votes or power.

2. It is the duty of all Catholics to plan and

labor for the absolute supremacy of the occupant of the chair of St. Peter.

3. It is the duty of all Catholics *"to take part in elections,"* and to know that *"politics are a part of morals. Politics are morals on the widest scale."* They must also give *"Perfect submission and obedience of will to the church and the sovereign Pontiff, as to God himself."* They must remember that they are to *"acknowledge no civil superior* before the holy father; that in their political work, *they must always and in the first place serve, as far as possible, the interests of Catholicism."*

4. We are opposed to any system of schools that teaches the youth more than the Roman Catechism, or that teaches the young to think—it is unnecessary, a waste of time and money, when the holy father has been deputed by God to do the thinking for this world. Therefore we call upon our subjects to do all possible to break down and destroy the free public schools of this heretical nation, which have compelled us to set up and maintain at great expense parochial schools to defend our faith, thus greatly lessening the income of the clergy.

5. We are in favor of filling all offices with men selected by the bishop of the diocese, upon whose political judgment all Catholics must rely, for the bishop *"must be obeyed whether right or*

wrong" [as Monsignor Preston testified under oath], and this is law. The faitful can confide in the bishop, though he may in one county or city compel you to support the candidates of one party, and in the next county or city support those of the other party, but you must not hesitate ; he "knows what he is doing," for in either case we get our glory and gain, and the holy church is the winner."

As the Romish church teaches that Catholics may kill Protestant heretics we should not be surprised at any conspiracy or plot they may devise in order to carry out their ends.

I will call attention to one case as a specimen of their work in our country, which doubtless is not generally known, viz; the assassination of President Lincoln. The charge was boldly made by Col. Edwin A. Sherman, in a public lecture in Boston, in which he gave a detailed account of it. From his statement, it seems that the hatred of the Romanists to Lincoln goes back to the time, previous to his nomination for the presidency, when he acted as counsel for ex-priest Father Chiniquy, in a civil suit, brought against him by his enemies, the Roman Catholics. After the trial was over he called on Lincoln to settle with him for his services.

Mr. Lincoln turned around and drew up a note,

and hearing sobbing behind him, he said, "Father Chiniquy, what are you crying about? You ought to be the happiest man alive. You have beaten all your enemies and come out triumphant; they have fled in disgrace, and you ought to be the happiest man alive." Father Chiniquy placed his hand upon his shoulder, and said; "I am not weeping for myself, but for you, sir. They will kill you; and let me tell you this, if I were in their place, and they in mine, it would be my solemn, sworn duty to take your life myself or find a man to do it."

Mr. Lincoln was continually in receipt of these threats of assassination from the time he entered into the defense of Father Chiniquy. He was continually warned from time to time, but at last, knowing that the opportunity was favorable, they could make use of the instrument, and Abraham Lincoln must die.

Of the men engaged in that conspiracy, Dr. Samuel Mudd was the chief director. He was a Roman Catholic, as was also John Wilkes Booth, Mrs. Surratt and her son; and in the judge advocate general's office at Washington, there may be seen the Roman Catholic medal taken from Booth's neck. A short time before that Booth had received the sacrament from Arch-bishop Spaulding, of Baltimore, and almost identically at the same time the pope sent from Rome the arms and accoutrements in exact counterpart of the papal guard at Rome, and when Archbishop Spaulding died, he was buried with military honors by the papal guard at Baltimore. In this conspiracy every one was a Roman Catholic, either a Jesuit, priest or layman, who made every effort to conceal it. I do not state this simply upon my own authority, but refer you to the official report of the trial before the military commission. Read it carefully, and you will find that all along the line it was for the interest of the Catholic church that even Mrs. Surratt should die. Her son, John B. Surratt, if he had been captured, would have been hung at the same time, but he had gotten the horse for Booth to escape, and waited until he heard the shot.

His escape had been prepared by Archbishop Bourget, of Montreal, Canada. He went there first, and returned to do part of his work, and he made his escape and was protected by that archbishop. He was placed in the charge of Father Charles Bougher of the parish of St. Leboire, Canada, there he kept him several months, finally he took him to Montreal, to another house of the archbishop, and there they kept him until they got ready to take him away. They took him in a carriage at Montreal to a small steamer which conveyed him down to Quebec, from whence he sailed on the steamer Peruvian to Liverpool, and thence to Havre de Grace, and from there went to Paris and Rome, and enlisted in the pope's body-guard. Rome now thought she had him secure, but through Father Chiniquy our government got track of him. A detective was put upon his track, and when the pope found that our government knew where he was, he made a pretense of being willing to give him up, but permitted him to make his escape. But he was captured at Alexandria, Egypt, and brought back on the United States war-ship Swatara, and tried in the court of the Dictrict of Columbia. It was a pity that the civil law had taken the place of the military. A jury that was never intended to agree was drawn, and this Jesuit priest, the accessory before and after the fact, so far as John H. Surratt was concerned, had the effrontery to come directly from Montreal, appear in that very court and give this very evidence I am now giving you; and if you turn to volume 2 of the trial of John H. Surratt, you will find all that I have said to you to be the exact truth. The investigation of this matter has been the work of years of the most patient research, and at an espense of thousands of dollars, mostly to myself and a few others. The hatred against Lincoln continued after his death. Among all the tributes of the nations of the earth, of societies and organizations, nearly one thousand that are bound in a book by the government, resolutions of sympathy and consolation, that came for the American people and among them were some from thirty and more Masonic lodges of Europe, supposing that he was a Mason, who draped their lodges in black, in France, Italy and elsewhere, yet you may examine that book from beginning to end—not from one single Roman Catholic society is there the first resolution of sorrow at this damnable act. Then, still farther, Rome determined to destroy all evidence, if possible. Her hatred goes into the ground. She believes in cremation from the beginning, but not of her own members, and to destroy the body of Lincoln she plotted its robbery. I had visited his tomb in 1876, at Springfield, Illinois, and saw the danger to which it was exposed, and there are some of us who have taken a solemn oath, (it rests upon us to-day,) not only to perpetuate his memory, but to preserve his remains."

"It became necessary to keep a guard there, but notwithstanding this precaution, they broke open the sarcophagus, ran out the cedar coffin, and were about to break into it when our friends were at hand. The ghouls were captured and every one was a Roman Catholic; they were tried and each sentenced to serve out his time in the state penitentiary of Illinois."

As confirmatory of the above statements, Walter Sims, in a lecture in Chicago, affirmed that "when young Surratt escaped, he went to Rome, where he was received, and when found by the American officers, was a member of the papal guards. Then when on trial at Washington, the priests sat with him, staring the jury in the face; and the students of the Jesuit college there, surrounded him, and said to the jury; 'The Roman Catholic Church gives him her protection;' therefore the jury did not agree."

There is one phase of Romanism that may not be overlooked is, the extortionate exactions upon the people for money, from the "Peter's pence" collected for the pope, down to the money demanded by the priests for baptisms and marriages, and for absolutions and masses, &c. And not content with these burdens, put upon the living, the dead even are taxed also, and when widows are called upon to pay money for masses to be said for the souls of their dead husbands. The following notice from a late paper will show that some of the dogmas of Romanism are not in harmony with the civil law of the land. "Some time ago a prominent Roman Catholic died in Mobile, and bequeathed $2,000 to be used for the masses for his soul." The court held the bequest void, because there was no living beneficiary of the trust endeavored to be created, the soul not being an entity in contemplation of the law."

I will now call attention to the indisputable fact that the pope is in the politics of this country. The lecturer quoted above well says that "The whole Roman Catholic church is moved by a button, which is pressed in Rome. The pope presses the button, and the cardinals are moved; the cardinals press the buttons and the bishops are moved, and so with the priests, who move the people; but the people have no buttons—theirs is simply to obey;" and as a result the Catholics will vote in obedience to the will of the pope, and of course he will require them to vote for such men and measures as will be most favorable to the Roman Catholic church. The Romish hierarchy is certainly the most far reaching despotism in this world. The statements previously made, as to the character of the Romish system, can be verified by reference simply to the highest dignitaries of the Romish Catholic church, some of which will here be given, as follows.

That the encyclical letter of Pope Leo XIII., written to American Catholics November 1, 1885, says: "We exhort all Catholics, who would devote careful attention to public matters, to take an active part in all municipal affairs and elections, and to favor the principles of the church in all public services, meetings and gatherings. All Catholics must make themselves felt as active elements in daily political life, in the countries where they live. They must penetrate, wherever possible, in the administration of civil affairs; must constantly exert the utmost vigilance and energy to prevent the usage of liberty from going beyond the limits of God's fixed laws. ALL CATHOLICS SHOULD DO ALL IN THEIR POWER TO CAUSE THE CONSTITUTIONS OF STATES, AND LEGISLATION TO BE MODELED IN THE PRINCIPLES OF THE TRUE CHURCH. All Catholic writers and journalists should never lose, for an instant, from view, the above prescriptions.

"It is not lawful to follow one rule in private conduct and another in the government of state, to wit: That the authority of the church should be observed in private life but rejected in state matters. *The Roman Church has the right to exercise its authority without any limit set to it by the civil powers.* The Pope and the priests ought to have dominion over temporal affairs; the Roman church and her ecclesiastics have a right to immunity from civil law. In case of conflict between ecclesiastical and civil powers the ecclesiastical ought to prevail."

That Cardinal Manning, speaking in the name of the Pope, said: "I acknowledge no civil power. I am the subject of no prince, and I claim more than this. I claim to be the supreme judge and director of the conscience of men, of the peasants that till the field and of the princes that sit upon the throne; of the household that lives in the shades of privacy, and the legislature that makes laws for kingdoms. I am the sole, last, supreme, judge of what is right or wrong."

That from 1855 to 1880 the Jesuits were driven from almost every civilized country on the globe, except from the United States, where they are now gradually weaving a net-work of their schemes from Maine to California, and from the Gulf to the interior of Canada.

That Pope, Pius IX., December 8th, 1864, said: "The Catholic religion, with all its VOTERS, ought to be exclusively dominant, in such sort, that every other worship should be banished and interdicted." He also said: "The church has the right to prevent the state from granting the public exercises of their own worship to persons emigrating into it."

"She has the power of requiring the state not to permit free expression of opinion.

The judicial functionaries must refuse obedience to the State and to the laws of the country which are in contradiction with Roman Catholic precepts."—*Syllabus of Pope Leo XIII.*

"But if the laws of the State are in open contradiction with the divine law, if they command anything prejudicial to the church, or are hostile to the duties imposed by religion, or violate in the person of the supreme pontiff the authority of Jesus Christ, then, indeed, it is a duty to resist them and a crime to obey them—a crime fraught with injury to the State itself."—*Allocution of Pope Leo XIII.*

"The Catholic religion, with all its votes, ought to be exclusively dominant in such sort that every other worship shall be banished and interdicted."—*Allocution of Pope Pius IX, September,* 1851.

"We can have the United States in ten years; and I want to give you three points for your consideration—the Indians, the negroes and the public schools."—*Archbishop Ireland, in a speech at Rome,* 1892.

"The absurd and erroneous doctrines, or ravings, in defense of liberty and conscience are a most pestilential error, a pest of all others to be dreaded in the State."—*Encyclical of Pope Pius XI, August* 15, 1854

"I hope that the Catholic hierarchy will be

worthy of this glorious country, which in the future it will religiously rule."—*Archbishop Ryan, of Philadelphia, at the annual dinner of the Catholic Club, February,* 1893.

"If Catholics ever gain a sufficient numerical majority in this country, religious freedom is at an end. So we say, so we believe."—*Editorial in the Shepherd of the Valley, official organ of Bishop Hughes, January* 26, 1852.

"No man has a right to choose his religion. Catholicism is the most intolerant of creeds. It is intolerance itself. We might as well rationally maintain that two and two do not make four as theory of religious liberty. Its impiety is only equaled by its absurdity."—*New York Freeman, official organ of Archbishop Hughes.*

"There is no other remedy for the evil but to put heretics to death."—*Cardinal Bellarmine.*

"Protestantism has not, and never can have, any rights where catholicity is triumphant."—*Catholic Review.*

"Let the public schools go where they came from—the devil."—*Freeman's Journal, December* 11, 1869.

"The Catholic church has a right to avail itself of force and to use the temporal power for that purpose."—*Encyclical* 24, *Pope Pius IX.*

"Roman Catholics must obey their bishops,

whether right or wrong."—*Thus swore Monsignor Preston on the witness stand in New York.*

"All legislation must be governed by the will of God, unerringly indicated by the pope."—*Priest Hecker, in the Catholic World, July.* 1870.

"Religious liberty is merely endured until the opposite can be carried into effect without peril to the catholic world."—*Bishop O'Connor, of Pittsburgh.*

Considering these sentiments coming from the highest Roman Catholic authorities, we cannot doubt what are the designs of the Romish Church toward our country, and what would be our condition should Romanism dominate here.

So it is not a matter of surprise that the pope of Rome should have the impudence to establish himself at the capital of our nation, in the person of the Italian Satolli. And here is his commission.

"We command all whom it concerns to recognize in you (Francisco Satolli) as apostolic delegate, *the supreme power* of the delegating pontiff: we command that they give you aid, concurrence, and obedience in all things, that they receive with reverence your salutary admonitions and orders. Whatever sentence or penalty you shall duly declare or inflict against those who oppose our authority, we will ratify, and, with the authority given us by the Lord, will cause to be observed inviolably until condign satisfaction be made." "*Notwithstanding constitutions and apostolic ordinance or other to the contrary.*"—Extract from encyclical of Pope Leo XIII, to the Papal clergy in the United States, January 24, 1892.

Of course one important part of his mission here was to figure in our politics, which is clearly revealed in the following extract of an open letter to him, from Bishop Coxe of New York.

MONSIGNOR: Your appearance in our city last November, less as a priest than a politician, was the occasion of my first letter to your excellency.

Once more I must remind you that you are an invader. You came among us in the week of our elections last autumn, an alien and an emissary, and made yourself a partaker in one of the most flagrant assaults upon our civil rights, and our domestic peace, that has ever disgraced American history.

The subversion of our municipal charter had culminated in the corruption of the shrievalty; in the appointment of ruffians as deputy sheriffs and policemen, to deprive honest Americans of franchise and to give it to aliens, by the browbeating and violence of mock magistrates, under forms of law. Among partisans of this sort you and your satellites were conspicuous. Of such "political workers," the chief offender was your orator and henchman. You were introduced as his ally; and in a city smarting with the wounds he had inflicted, you read us a lecture on our Constitution, as you and he understand it; and you also dilated upon the character of our Washington, displaying your ignorance of both these important matters, as also of the language in which the Constitution is written.

Emboldened by that day's work, and not ashamed, you proceeded without delay to proclaim your policy with reference to our public schools. I was amazed that no public man remonstrated, when, after such interference with American institutions, you announced your permanent residence in Washington, as if you were an accredited ambassador, assuming precedence in the diplomatic corps. You were, in diplomatic terms, a *persona non grata* to the patriotic sentiment of the whole nation.

Unrecognized and unaccredited, you parade yourself as the lawful representative of a "court" which has no nationality to justify it in claiming international relations of any kind. You have not less insulted Americans of your own religion, by accepting a supremacy over local dignitaries, which it is announced that no American citizen will be allowed to exercise. You are simply a missionary of the Jesuit sect, coming here to propagate your intolerant ideas as I have quoted them, from the "Pustet Catechism." I might quote them to the horror and dismay of good men, from the authorized "Morality," Liguori and the offensive teachings of the Jesuits, exposed by Pascal in the "Provincial Letters." I have asked you in vain to refute me, if possible, by calling upon your "university" in Washington, to give us a faithful translation of the *breve* of Clement XIV. He tells us, under the "Ring of the Fisherman," what knaves and assassins Jesuits are, even among their co-religionists. I have also invited you to enlighten us by a similar translation of the "Secret Instructions" of the Jesuit society. Of these instructions a learned friend secured an authentic copy in Italy, which has never been printed, and which he has placed at my disposal." Other prominent ministers, and others have used some very strong language in reference to Romanism, and I will let them speak for themselves.

The *Tennessee Methodist* speaks with no uncertain sound on the question of Romanism. It says:

"We hear a great deal from radically conservative Protestant papers about 'American Catholicism,' 'the liberalizing effects of our institutions on Rome,' 'the progressive and liberal wing of Romanism,' and much more of such nonsense. There is just enough of truth in these statements to make them exceedingly dangerous. Let it be remembered, always, that there is just as much 'liberalism' in the Romish church *as Romanists are compelled to feign from purely political considerations*—that in order to reach a controlling power in this or any other country, they are willing to seem to make almost any sort of concessions to the spirit of the age, and to the institutions which surround them. But once in power they quickly cast off all such masks, and we find the same old relentless, sleepless foe to free government, which has sought dominion for long ages—the same repressing, stifling, blighting influence, which seeks to check human progress, and remand proud civilizations back to the crudities and darkness of medievalism.

"In arts of deception she always excelled. There are no limitations to her lengths in this nefarious practice, for one of the cardinal principles on which she operates is that 'the end justifies the means'—a principle as base and as destructive of righteousness, and as fruitful of diabolicism of all sorts, as Satan could possibly desire.

"It is painful, indeed, to witness the number of Protestants who are duped by the Romish Church, who send children to her schools and talk glibly of her 'liberalism,' and fondly dream that they are toying with a thing different from the monster which could produce a St. Bartholomew in 1572. The day hastens when they will be undeceived. When you patronize in any way, however remotely, the Romish Church, you are aiding a sworn enemy to your own church, and abetting a powerful and superbly organiz d rebellion against your Government and your individual liberties."

"*That* Rev. Byron Sunderland, pastor of the First Presbyterian Church, at Washington, at which Mr. and Mrs. Cleveland are attendants, said, in a recent sermon:

"The battle with the papacy is yet to come, and may even now be at our doors. We cannot afford to have the functions of this government paralyzed by the decrees of a foreign potentate. We are rapidly reaching 100,000,000 of people over an area of 3,000,000 square miles. Our nation is polyglot, foreign elements are multiplying among us, and there is one element which is palpably irreconcilable with the spirit and design of our institutions, whatever may be the professions of its more liberal adherents, and that is the Roman papacy.

"An order of men is harbored among us—men who have been expelled at one time and another from every civilized country under heaven; and that order is the Jesuits, who are free to circulate among the people, and who don't hesitate to declare that this Protestant nation shall one day reckon with the Roman pontiff. We have had our battles on various vital questions in the past, but the battle with the papacy is yet to come, and may even now be at the doors."

The *Christian Inquirer* speaks:

"When the people do wake from the long and guilty sleep, the public indignation will be so great that the whole relations of the State to this foreign church will change. The time is not far away when 40,000,000 Protestants will no longer allow the 8,000,000 Romanists, led largely by foreign priests, taking their politics from Rome, to hold so much power and draw so largely on the public treasury as at present. The Church of Rome in America is overdoing the thing altogether, and the reaction is as certain as the revolution of the seasons. When the inevitable conflict comes, it will be short, sharp, decisive. Whether it be at the ballot box or in the streets it will soon end. It will be 40,000,000 against 8,000,000."

The Roman Catholic Church is not merely a religious, but a political organization, and the pope a monster despot, and the danger to our republic lies, not in the proselyting of our native born population by Romish priests to the Catholic faith, but from unrestricted emigration, by which Roman Catholic countries continue to transfer to our country "the dregs of their population," representing the lowest forms of illiteracy, beggary, superstition and crime. And mark a significant fact, that "while the Catholics number only about one seventh of the population of the United States, they have contributed more criminals, and paupers, than have been contributed by all outside of the Catholic Church."

And now, the question is not whether one or the other of the political parties of our country shall dominate, but whether Protestantism or Romanism shall prevail; in other words, whether we shall enjoy civil and religious liberty, or be required to think and believe as a foreign pope shall dictate.

I will here make a statement which ought to be a startling one to every friend of our country. No real Roman Catholic, can be a true citizen of this Republic. If he seeks citizenship here, he must take the oath of allegiance, and he is required to make oath "to renounce forever all allegiance and fidelity to any foreign prince, potentate, state, or sovereignty, in particular that to which he has been subject." And as the religion of the Catholic requires of him supreme allegiance to the pope of Rome, if he continues to be a Catholic, he lives a lie and will swear to one whenever it suits his purpose; in fact the canon law of the Romish Church requires that "no oath is to be kept toward heretics, or Protestants," and that "the pope can absolve from all oaths;" and so their oaths of allegiance to the government of the United States is not worth the snap of the finger.

The fact is, Catholics are allowed to kill heretics, as a good, pious act, and murder or any other crime is justifiable in the case of Protestants, on the satanic principle that "the end justifies the means." So the religion of a cardinal, bishop or priest allows them to play the hypocrite or swear a lie whenever the interest of the Catholic Church requires it. And such is the class of persons who are admitted to the right of suffrage in this country of ours. The statements made here are sustained by the facts, adduced in the preceding pages.

It is a notorious fact that the government of

New York city, by the Tammany ring, has been under the control of the Roman Catholics, and that no city on this continent has ever exceeded it in the corrupt and criminal practices of its officials; and the outrages became so glaring that on the eve of the late election, the ministers from the pulpits exhorted their people to go to the ballot box and, without regard to any political party, oust the thieving and black mailing criminals from office.

There is no doubt that the Romish hierarchy have in operation all of their Jesuitical machinery, and are using the *subtlety* of the devil in order to establish in this country the despotism of Leo the 13th; and doubtless the final conflict is fast approaching which will decide the question whether Romanism or Protestantism shall dominate in these United States.

The Romish prelates are making war on our free schools, scheming to control elections, and are forming secret military companies, and with the hordes of foreign Catholic emigrants continually pouring into our country, no doubt they hope for a favorable time soon to arrive when they can subjugate our country to Romanism.

My attention has been recently called to a circular addressed to the people, issued by a number of prominent citizens of Washington city, embracing several of the city pastors, and headed by the Pastor of the Metropolitan Baptist Church of that city. The object of the address is to urge upon the voters of the country the necessity of electing such men as our representatives, without regard to party, who will pass laws to restrict emigration, prevent the appropriation of thousands of dollars by the government, as has been done, for the support of Roman Catholic Indian Schools, and other institutions entirely under the control of Roman Catholics.

And statements are made, which go to show that the Roman Catholics have a controlling influence over the United States government. Besides the fact that Roman Catholics have been, under the present administration, appointed to foreign missions; as postmasters in some of our largest cities; as collectors of Revenue, and large numbers of them to office in the different departments at Washington, the following statements are made in regard to the Romish hierarchy:

"It has established in the city of Washington a 'Bureau of Catholic Indian Missions,' an ecclesiastical political machine of the most offensive character. It is a standing menace to the peace of the republic; it is run on the most approved Jesuitical methods; it is unscrupulous,

It is organized for public plunder. It dominates the Indian office; it intimidates Congress and dictates to the present administration of the National Government. It has taken millions of dollars from the public treasury, and to-day has free access to the vaults. The Indian bill now before Congress carries an appropriation of large sums of money for this papal pirate, in violation of the spirit and letter of the Constitution and against the formal protests of multitudes of citizens who are outraged and robbed by it. The bill will be enacted into law by a Democratic Congress in payment of political services and with the consent of truculent Republicans who barter principles for votes."

"*That* the majority of judges of our Court of Appeals, the highest judicial body in the District of Columbia, are Roman Catholics."

I will here state some facts which were introduced in a speech before the last Congress by Mr. Linton of Michigan, against the bill to appropriate money for Sectarian schools, which affords a specimen of some work the Jesuits are doing at Washington. The speaker presented statistics showing that during a number of years past the Roman Catholics have received from the government more than three millions of dollars for the support of their schools, or more than all the

Protestant denominations put together; and in addition to this the statement was made that "the Roman Catholic school at Devil's Lake was in a Government building, and when the training school was established at Fort Totten, the sister's school was made part of the Government school, and the sisters retained as teachers under Government pay.

Now mark the action taken by the Protestant denominations of our country. The Gen. Conference of the Methodist Episcopal Church of 1892, adopted the following resolutions. "Whereas, the appropriation of public funds for sectarian purposes by the National Government is not only wrong in principle, but in violation of both the letter and spirit of the Constitution of the United States: Therefore, Resolved, that this General Conference of the Methodist Episcopal Church requests the Missionary Societies working under its sanction or control, to decline either to petition for or to receive from the National Government any moneys for educational work among the Indians."

Similar action has also been taken by the following Protestant denominations, viz; the General Assembly of the Presbyterian, and the United Presbyterian Church, the General Convention of the Prot. Episcopal Church, and the American

Missionary Association of the Congregational Church. Besides these may be named "the Baptist denomination, that has never accepted, but always refused, this public money for their Missionary work.

Now, in view of the fact that all of the leading Protestant denominations of the United States have refused to receive any Government appropriations in violation of the Constitution, leaving the Government to appropriate hundreds of thousands of dollars to schools under Roman Catholic control, and while these Jesuits are entrenched at Washington, with their great University, and Bureau of Indian Schools, carrying on their lobbying schemes to influence legislation in favor of the Romish Church; and while these facts were brought before the last Congress and disregarded, the language of a speaker was appropriate if not prophetic, when he said: "I do not believe the Congress of the United States can long stand upon the ground we occupy to-day. There is already a gathering storm, and that storm may break before a great while upon the Congress and the people of the United States." And now, it is a historical fact that a storm has come, and swept away that Congress, and it has gone to "where the woodbine twineth, and the whang-doodle mourneth for his first born."

"Meek-appearing nuns stand in the passage-ways of the Department buildings on pay days, and in that appealing manner known only to a professional Romish beggar, solicit, with outstretched hands, contributions, the employees fearing not to give, lest, through the priestly influence behind the powers in Washington, they should lose their situations. A whisper against the papacy would simply cost them their positions. Watchmen and messengers, whose foreign brogue easily discloses their nationality, act as 'cappers' and spies, and what they see and hear is promptly reported to the priest in charge of that particular Department. The appointing clerks in the War, Navy, State, Interior, and probably in other Departments, are Romanists, whose business it is to see to it that their kind receive the favors at their disposal. The same priestly influence controls the government of the Capital City to a dangerous extent. The public schools of the District of Columbia are fast filling up with Roman Catholic teachers. Liquor licenses are freely granted to Romanists, who flagrantly violate the laws prohibiting the opening of saloons within 400 feet of a church or school building. These things are not conjectures—they are facts.

"Priests frequent the lobbies and hang about the committee rooms like so many harpies, while

'Father' Stephan is seen moving around and button-holing members of Congress on important occasions.

"Rome orders the rejection of an American nominee for the Supreme Bench, and it is done. Cardinal Gibbons pays but two visits to the White House; a Jesuit is selected for that high position, and is confirmed within two hours after his appointment without a dissenting voice.

"Statues of eminent Roman Catholics are being placed in Statuary Hall in the Capitol building.

"A statue of the Pope himself adorns the grounds of the 'American Vatican' in the District of Columbia.

"The mansion of the 'American Pope,' Satolli, overlooks the Capitol of the United States. Roman Catholic soldiers, bearing arms, escort the Pope's Ablegate to and from the trains that waft his precious person in and out of the city, upon his missions throughout the country, teaching treasonable doctrines of supreme obedience to his master at Rome, while from the flagstaff over his residence or upon the grounds adjacent floats the banner of the Papacy."

That such a state of things can exist at the seat of government of a Protestant Republic, and that the interests of our country are placed in the hands of so many Roman Catholic Jesuits, we must believe that partisan politics have become, so corrupted that the Catholic vote *has been bought, and paid for!* For further information I refer to Rev. Green Clay Smith, Washington, D. C.

And considering these things, ought not every Protestant voter to be aroused, and go to the polls hereafter, and vote for such men only to administer our government as will not bow the knee to a foreign pope, and give aid and comfort to these Jesuitical enemies of ours?

In conclusion, if any one should dissent from my exposition of the 17th chapter of Revelation, and its application to the papacy, my reply is, if it does not refer to that great hierarchy, what does it refer to? I challenge any one to name any organization on earth that has more, or as many, marks of identity with the woman described as "sitting upon the scarlet colored beast," as does the papacy, or better fill the description of the apostates referred to by the apostle Paul as holding the doctrines of devils, and specifying one of them as "forbidding to marry."

And before dismissing the subject I will call attention to the fact, that the woman representing the papacy was named "Babylon," and in Rev. chapter 18th is a history of *her fall*, under the same name, and in the same figurative language. If this view be correct, then we may hope for the destruction of the great Romish hierarchy. God speed the day when the announcement shall be made according to his Word, that "Babylon the great is fallen, is fallen!" I submit what I have written to my readers, challenging investigation, in the light of the scriptures, and of authentic history. Yet I have not used up all the ammunition at command, and can load up and fire a few more guns if necessary.

P. S.—Perhaps it is a hereditary thing with me to look with horror upon the Roman Catholic Church, as from childhood it has been associated in my mind with persecutions and bloodshed. My ancestors, the French Huguenots, were the subjects of her cruel persecutions. Susannah Rochette, the Huguenot girl, after the massacre of St. Bartholomew, escaped to Holland as a refugee, being carried on ship-board, after night, concealed in a hogshead. She afterward married a French refugee, Abram Michaux, and they emigrated to Virginia. Their son was my great grandfather, and while their remains repose in the old cemetery on James River, above Richmond, and while I live, will I oppose the intolerant and persecuting Church of Rome.

www.ingramcontent.com/pod-product-compliance
Lightning Source LLC
Chambersburg PA
CBHW031735230426
43669CB00007B/354